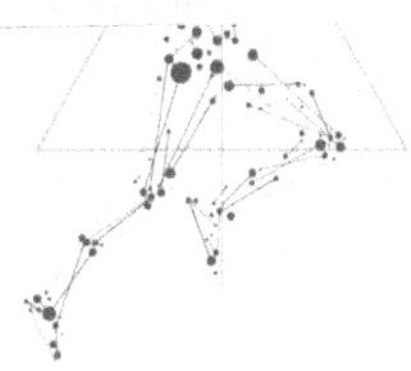

What people are saying

'This book provides a valuable framework on how to get the best out of ourselves in a balanced and meaningful way. Particularly, the re-evaluation of priorities and the ability to reconnect with the important things in life.'

Dr John F. Kelly

Dr Kelly is the Elizabeth R. Spallin Professor of Psychiatry in the Field of Addiction Medicine at Harvard Medical School – the first endowed professor in addiction medicine at Harvard. He's the founder and Director of the Recovery Research Institute at Massachusetts General Hospital (MGH) and the Associate Director of the Center for Addiction Medicine at MGH.

'I wish they taught some of these fundamentals in school as many of the skills and learnings covered can make all the difference when it comes to achieving our goals.'

Simon Pond

Simon is a former Major League Baseball player and Olympian. His career spanned 13 years as a professional baseball player.

'An enjoyable and thought-provoking read which explores and deepens our understanding of what success means to each of us.'

Patrick Haughey

TV and radio producer with RTE and Today FM, Patrick has been a senior producer on many shows in the business and current affairs arena such as *The Last Word* with Matt Cooper (Today FM) and RTE's *The Big Bite* with David McWilliams.

THE SUCCESS COMPLEX

ADRIAN KELLY

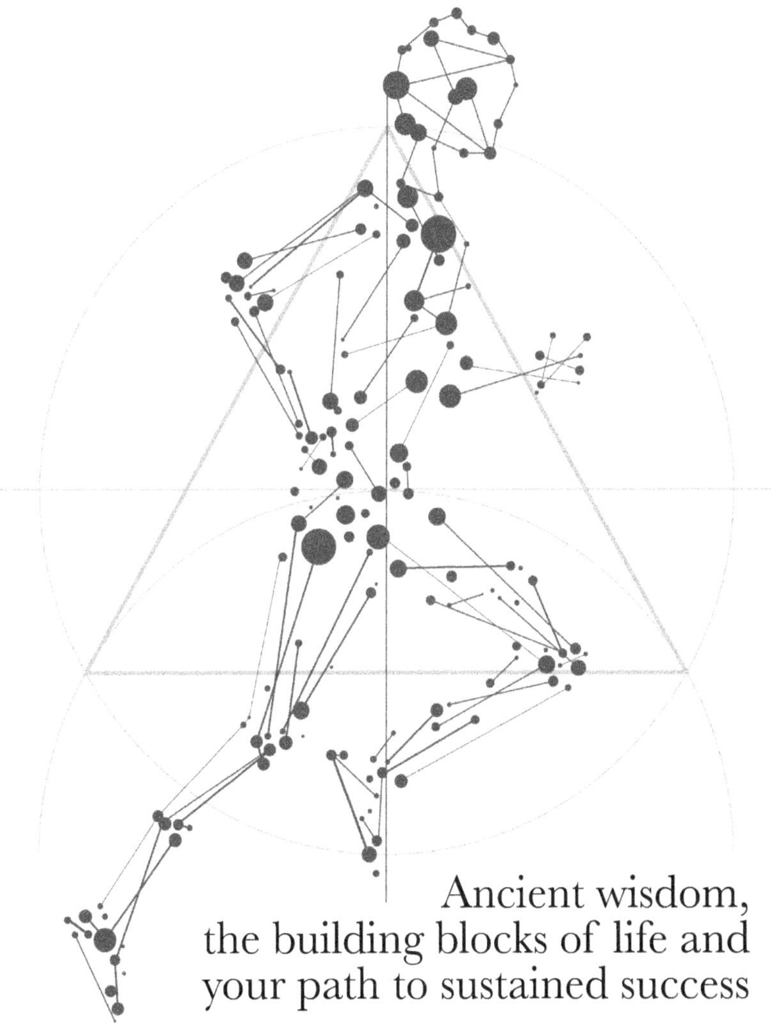

Ancient wisdom,
the building blocks of life and
your path to sustained success

First published in Great Britain by Practical Inspiration Publishing, 2024

ISBN 978-1-78860-593-9 (hardback)
978-1-78860-379-9 (paperback)
978-1-78860-381-2 (epub)
978-1-78860-380-5 (mobi)

Want to bulk-buy copies of this book for your team and colleagues? We can customize the content and co-brand The Success Complex to suit your business's needs.

Please email info@practicalinspiration.com for more details.

I'd like to dedicate this book to my wife Mary Brigid and my children Amelia, Laurence, Leo and Rosemary. Thank you for your support, patience and inspiration. And to my parents, particularly my mother, Mary, who we sadly lost at a young age, and my father, Stan, who died last year.

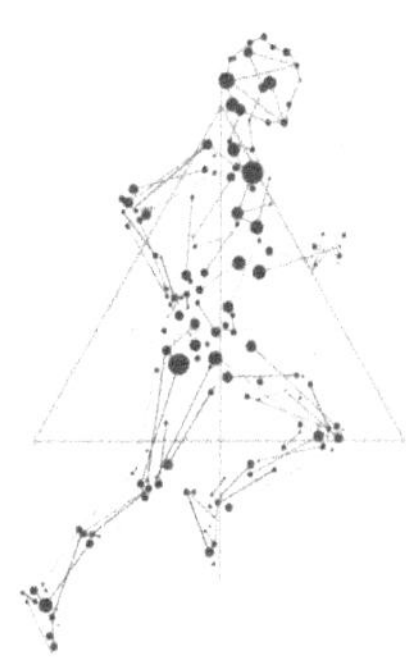

Contents

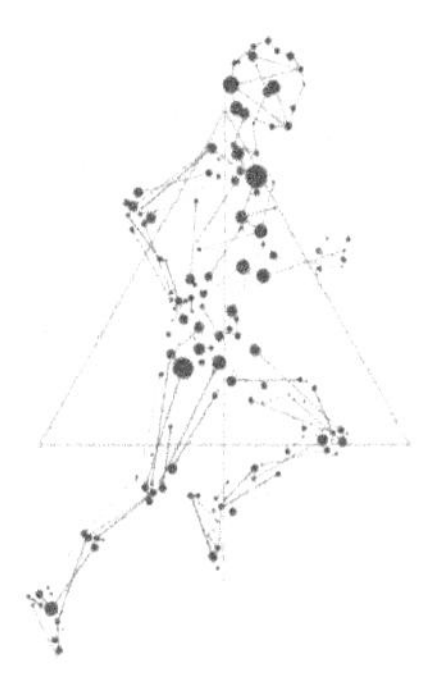

Acknowledgements

There are so many people whose thoughts and insights have shaped this book. To all of you out there, I'm profoundly grateful. This is an attempt to thank as many as possible.

Firstly, thank you to the Practical Inspiration Publishing team and our design and production partners Newgen Publishing UK for their patience and understanding as I missed deadlines here and there. Working with you has been a pleasure.

A special thanks to the boss at Practical Inspiration Publishing, Alison Jones, for her encouragement, guidance and belief in the initial idea that became this book.

This book found its first expression in interviews I conducted with friends and colleagues in a variety of fields. Interviews that probed the questions I wanted answers to. In particular, I thank mentors in my life such as my older brother John and my father Stan. I also want to say a special word of thanks to my uncle, Leo Kelly, who went out of his way, particularly in challenging times, to provide support, encouragement and inspiration, always accompanied by his trademark good humour. What we found together, through these many conversations, are an abundance of tools and guidance that I hope will help the reader to find your own success in life, whatever that might be. It's a book of ideas and insights, many of which I hope will help the people who need a little support with whatever challenge they might face.

In particular I want to give a huge thank you to all those who reviewed the material and gave valuable feedback, including in no particular order:

Mark Quinn, Jackie Ward, Simon Pond, Fergal McManus, Tom Kelley, Cian McMahon, Claire Mason, Lisa Cresswell, Sharon Magennis, Aaron Flynn, Ulick Burke, Shane O'Connor, Dermot O'Reilly, Brian Lynch, Martin O'Hart, Emmet Colleran, Prof. Kevin Mitchell, Prof. David Eddie, Dr John F. Kelly, Dr Ken Van Someren, Dr Janine Van Someren, Marcus Magee, Commandant Richie Barber, Patrick Haughey, Sean Cavanagh, Darren Hughes, Colin Morgan, Darren Greenan, Ben Folkman and many others who I apologize for missing by name, but you know who you are; and finally all my business colleagues at BNI Rossmore.

I would also, of course, like to thank my supportive, hard-working and knowledgeable wife Mary Brigid and my kids for their patience, understanding and inspiring curiosity.

Finally, thank you to all my guests on *The Success Complex* podcast for helping me explore writing so thoughtfully and generously, and to all those who listen and support the ongoing search for important answers to life's questions.

Go raibh míle maith agaibh.

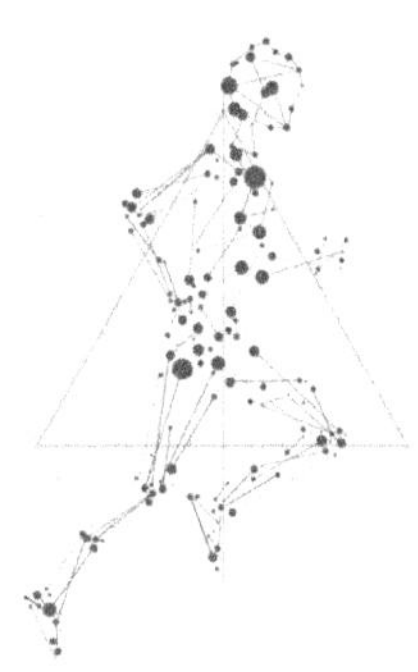

Introduction

This book is about a complex we might have that stops us achieving our objectives in life. It refers to a complex in the sense of a fear of heights, small spaces and so on. It could be something we can't put our finger on, an invisible force that thwarts our efforts. The objective here is to shed light on the sort of things we sometimes miss that can make all the difference.

When we think of challenges and learning new skills, memories of riding a bicycle for the first time may spring to mind. I had great fun teaching my four kids how to master the art of the bicycle on the sloping incline to our house. Every child learns differently, of course, and despite my success with three of my older kids the local school did a much better job teaching my youngest daughter how to ride a bicycle.

Cast your mind back for a moment to when you first tried to ride a bicycle. You were expected to take your feet off the ground and place them on the pedals. What seems easy now was terrifying as a child. Every time you tried to do this, the bicycle would lurch to one side, and if you didn't get a foot down to rebalance, you could hit the ground hard, with this heavy, clumsy apparatus on top of you.

For example, inventor and bike enthusiast Ryan McFarland had similar difficulty teaching his son to ride a bike. A common approach is to attach more apparatus to a bicycle, such as additional stabilizing wheels.

The key skills we need to develop, however, include learning weight distribution, balance and the importance of momentum. The addition of stabilizing wheels isn't the most efficient means of teaching these skills because they actually negate the need for such things as balance and momentum.

McFarland saw this difficulty and simplified the approach. He took away the pedals and lowered the centre of gravity so that the child could easily keep their balance using each foot, and use their feet for momentum, building confidence and teaching these vital skills. He essentially simplified the approach, in order to focus on the things that would really make a difference.

In this book we'll take a journey through history to explore pivotal events and people, with the benefit of modern-day behavioural science as a touchstone. We'll do this to explore what we can learn to help us on our journey.

We'll also use the principles of balance and momentum to structure the book's framework.

Part 1 includes seven chapters on core skills represented by the letter ***A*** for activity or actions that we can take to address challenges in our lives, whether sought out or thrust upon us. Part 2 examines a ***B***alance to be struck in applying ourselves and these skills in a sustained way, regarding personal values and the avoidance of burnout. Part 3 explores a point of ***C***ongruence. A meeting of points A and B. A direction we might find worthwhile moving towards an optimal point C, which is personal and unique to all of us as individuals. Things we could probably do with a little more of in our lives.

In *The Success Complex*, essentially I want to do for our understanding of these challenges what McFarland did for the bicycle.

Part 1
Activity

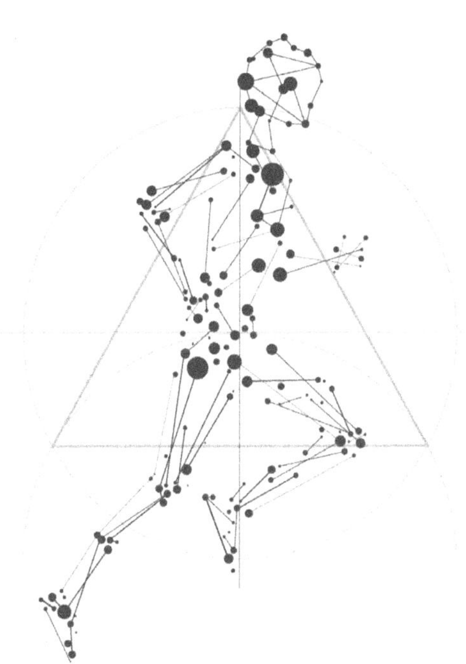

1

Imagining the Impossible

'If you define the problem correctly, you almost have the solution.'

Steve Jobs[1]

It was a rescue attempt that involved c.10,000 people, c.2,000 soldiers, c.900 police officers, c.700 diving cylinders used by c.90 divers (c.50 of whom were foreign nationals who had travelled to Thailand to help), ten police helicopters and seven ambulances. But in the end it all came down to just one conversation.

Twelve children and their football coach had become trapped in an air pocket of a cave filled with water, about four kilometres from the entrance. The year was 2018 and the place Tham Luang Nang Non cave, Chiang Rai Province in northern Thailand.

On 23 June 2018, the children, aged between 11 and 16, and their 25-year-old coach decided to explore the cave system as part of a birthday celebration for one of their players. They entered the cave and subsequently got lost, becoming trapped by rapidly rising flood waters as Thailand entered its rainy

[1] C. Azzari, *Top 22 inspirational quotes on finding a solution*, The Daily SEM (28 August 2020). Available from https://thedailysem.com/top-22-inspirational-quotes-on-finding-a-solution/

season. The group walked deep into the cave system to find higher ground, and ended up trapped.

A tremendous rescue effort began, which included damming off rivers flowing into the cave system and pumping over a billion litres of water from the cave over the course of the rescue. This was 'the equivalent of approx. 48 Olympic-sized swimming pools in a 75-hour period'.[2]

Despite the presence of highly skilled military teams such as Thai Navy seals and the US Navy Pararescue service, the divers didn't have the equipment or the experience to reach the stricken group.

It was decided to source help from the world's foremost experts on cave diving. These included Richard Stanton and John Volanthen, UK-based amateur cave-diving enthusiasts. To state the obvious, Stanton and Volanthen were not what the military personnel were used to seeing on rescue missions. They were two middle-aged English men accustomed to wearing shorts and flip-flops and applying a laid-back approach to life. They did, however, have the rare skills and equipment the other rescue teams did not.

Incredibly, eight days after the group became trapped they were located by Stanton and Volanthen, who had pushed themselves and their oxygen supplies to the limit. The group were in surprisingly good mental and physical health.

It took the two divers 11 hours to make the remarkable eight-kilometre round trip under water. After the news filtered through to the outside world, the initial elation and celebration gave way to the sober enormity of the task that lay ahead.

It's difficult to exaggerate the difficulty of extracting the trapped group. All alternatives were being considered, such as finding new cave entrances, drilling a shaft from above the cave and supplying the group with food until the rainy season ended in October. All of these, particularly the latter, were too risky given the potential for further rises in water levels and their dangerously low oxygen levels.

Pumping the water out of the cave was also being assessed as a prospect but, despite pumping rates of 1.6 million litres per hour, the water level was only

---

[2] J. Lange, *7 incredible facts about the Thai cave rescue*, https://theweek.com/speedreads/783973/7-incredible-facts-about-thai-cave-rescue (10 July 2018).

going down by one centimetre per hour. And that was after it had *stopped* raining.

Supplying the group with diving gear and having them swim out underwater beside experienced divers was also deemed impossible.

Stanton and Volanthen had just a few days earlier rescued some adult pump workers in the same cave system. They had become stranded not far from the entrance. The pump workers, who had no diving experience, were given 'diving regulator mouthpieces' to breathe through and were accompanied by Stanton and Volanthen individually until they had reached the cave's entrance. As John describes it, they 'could not even hold it together for 30 seconds without panicking'.[3] These were adults, and they probably would have drowned if the journey out had taken more than a few minutes.

In the minds of Stanton and Volanthen, who were preparing to leave the country, the rescue was clearly *impossible*. A 'never say die' US Air Force sergeant, Derek Anderson, however, wanted to know one thing from them both before they left Thailand: what did the 'impossible look like'?[4]

In this chapter, we'll explore how impossible situations can sometimes bring out the very best in us. We'll delve into the art of creating space for innovation, by suspending the grip of glaring obstacles and instead finding a new starting point. A starting point at the sometimes fantastical, winning end result.

Defining the problem correctly

If we consider our Steve Jobs quote at the beginning of this chapter, it really comes down to teasing out what the correct question is. In the high-octane business world, identifying the right question to ask can be key to solving complex problems.

---

[3] G. Kiladay, 'Nat Geo doc films embarks on Thai cave rescue project directed by Kevin Macdonald (exclusive).' *The Hollywood Reporter* (4 March 2019).

[4] Ibid. See interview with Sergeant Derek Anderson.

In 1950s America, Robert McNamara (senior executive and later president of the Ford motor company) had a problem to solve.[5] During the war years the company had barely broken even, financially. Furthermore, during the 1950s, they were leaking market share to new competitors in the US, such as Volkswagen.

No one could give him basic information (by today's standards) on the profiles of customers buying cars. Therefore, McNamara set up the first market research department and said to his senior executives, 'Find out who in the hell is buying the Volkswagens.'[6] He quickly found out that they were professors, doctors, lawyers and people who could financially afford more. The question ultimately became: was there a market Ford were missing?

This question led Ford to a largely untapped market for affordable cars – which no one would have believed was there. The common opinion was that people wanted bigger cars, not smaller ones. However, by pinpointing the current consumer profile, McNamara found a group with an unaddressed need: those who couldn't afford Ford's current offering. So the new Ford Falcon was designed with a lighter body, smaller engine (95 HP) and overall reduced price tag.

This resulted in record sales for Ford. Over half a million new Ford Falcons were sold in the first year, and over a million sold by the end of the second year.[7]

It also changed the industry and saw a new focus on affordability, signalling the end for several over-sized car models in the 1950s. What's impressive here is the ability to ask the right question. This involves taking stock of a situation, pushing yourself and your team in a sometimes unknown and uncomfortable direction, but the results tend to speak for themselves. With this in mind let's return to the important question that Sergeant Derek Anderson thought to ask.

---

[5] McNamara of course also went on to become Secretary for Defense and later President of the World Bank.

[6] See *'Get the data'*: E. Morris, director, *The Fog of War: Eleven Lessons from the Life of Robert S. McNamara*, Sony Pictures Classics (2003). Available from www.sonypictures.com/movies/thefogofwar

[7] *Ford Falcon Summary*, Ford Falcon Registry. Available from www.falconregistry.com/history/summary.php [accessed 21 March 2024].

What did the impossible look like?

The answer given by Stanton and Volanthen to Sergeant Derek Anderson was that, as divers, they would need to be in control of an inanimate package in order to be able to deliver it through a four-kilometre cave system under water. Particularly given the fact that some of the underwater passageways on the route to the cave exit were less than 15 inches in diameter.

Considering this strange proposal, the question then became: in what circumstance would it be possible to put the members of the trapped group to sleep for the duration of the journey out of the cave system?

Impossible dream

To push ourselves to find new solutions and think creatively we sometimes have to cast our minds across a chasm of disbelief. To do this is to directly project your mind to the solution, regardless of how impossible it might seem, and then work backwards.

Shifting to the world of chess for a moment, former Irish number one and International Master, Mark Quinn, describes this creative and solution-oriented process as 'building a reverse-engineered bridge to the solution and then working backwards'. Quinn has spent over four decades visualizing solutions in the complex game of chess.

In chess, visualizing an ideal outcome and reverse-engineering the solution can be very effective, just like in real-life situations. An effective attack on the chess king usually involves identifying and taking out the key defensive pieces that are facilitating its protection. This means, metaphorically, standing on the solution side of the proposed 'reverse-engineered bridge' and looking back across to plot each step of the way across that bridge.

Returning to the real-world cave rescue situation in Thailand, another hero steps into the fold. Dr Richard Harris, an Australian anaesthetist and cave diver, who was contacted by Volanthen to see whether their idea was possible.[8] At first, Dr Harris was dismissive of the idea, given the dangers involved: 'My immediate response was absolutely not… I could think of 100

---

[8] Dr Richard Harris was later awarded Australian of the Year 2019 for his efforts in the Tham Luang Nang cave rescue.

ways a child could die in this scenario. For example, you need to maintain the airway; simply not keeping their chin up could result in asphyxiation.'[9]

Reluctantly, Dr Harris agreed to go to Thailand to *at least* assess the situation. His assessment was that the anaesthetic would have to be administered not just once, but twice during the arduous two-and-a-half-hour dive out of the cave system. It would also have to be administered by an untrained medical person during the dive. In other words, by the experienced diver traversing the cave system with their unconscious passenger.

Nothing like this had ever been done before. Dr Harris was later warned by the Australian diplomatic officials in Thailand that were he to oversee such a proposed sedation of the children and it went wrong, he could end up in a Thai prison. The risks were incredible and the chances of this plan working out were slim.

So, what drove them on?

Interestingly, despite the heroics of finding the children, a task that would be seen by many as contribution enough to the rescue, Volanthen described how things changed for him at that point. He felt the responsibility, despite it not officially being on his shoulders, was 'morally on my shoulders'.[10] After Dr Harris dived down and met the kids and their coach, he felt the same way.

Ultimately, they couldn't rest until they had done everything they could to rescue those kids, even though Dr Harris was risking prison and felt that it was almost a euthanasia situation – sparing them a death of starvation, drowning or asphyxiation as a result of their current scenario. The downsides of this not working out were simply horrific.

Let's take a moment here to appreciate a fascinating truth: it's precisely the sheer scale of a challenge that can ignite the flames of remarkable innovation.

They were successful, and a few days after they entered the cave to implement the plan, all of the group were rescued and in good health. Words cannot do justice to this incredible achievement of teamwork, innovation and calculated

---

[9] See interview with Dr Richard Harris. 'Nat Geo doc films embarks on Thai cave rescue project directed by Kevin Macdonald (exclusive).' *The Hollywood Reporter* (4 March 2019).

[10] Ibid.

risk-taking. None of this would have been possible if they hadn't opened their minds to the possibilities.

How can we use this in the broader context?

Overcoming indifference and becoming invested in making the right decision involves challenging ourselves. Asking what we're capable of. I commonly speak with students who have all sorts of ambitions.

When projecting forward as to what one future career might hold for you over another, it's worth considering the perspective of French astronaut Thomas Pesquet. One of the few astronauts to have spent more than one year in space, Pesquet described recently how he dreamed of becoming an astronaut as a child. 'It was very naive at the time, I had no idea how to become an astronaut, there is no straight path… there's no astronaut school, there's no exam you can pass to make you become an astronaut.' They're 'only doing one astronaut selection process every 10 to 15 years in Europe.'[11]

At the beginning it certainly looked like an impossible task. What's really interesting though, is his approach to solving this problem.

Pesquet goes on to say in the same interview: 'You have to build your career by blocks.' He describes how he first became an aerospace engineer. He then became a pilot. It's fair to say that each 'block', as he describes it, had its own rewards and sense of achievement. Each block broadened his skill sets, his opportunities and his horizons in the world, regardless of achieving his ultimate outcome, which he concedes had an element of luck; that is, being in the 'right place at the right time'. We explore the concept of positioning ourselves to be luckier in later chapters.

Summary

Perhaps the key in dealing with seemingly impossible challenges is to allow the time and space to divine the right question to ask.

---

[11] 'Leaders with Lacqua: Pesquet's lifelong journey to space', *Bloomberg Markets and Finance* (March 2022).

This involves a process of gathering together, where possible, the right skill sets, experience and information to refine the questions, until we're comfortable that we're asking the right one. Often this entails prodding and poking the challenge itself to exhaustively define the key issue. When that work is done it's productive to shift perspectives to the solution end of the metaphorical bridge.

This often releases us from the grip of immediate obstacles and allows our mind to float untethered to a necessary altitude where solutions can be found to what we thought was impossible, and with the right expertise we can translate this into practical and world-class problem-solving.

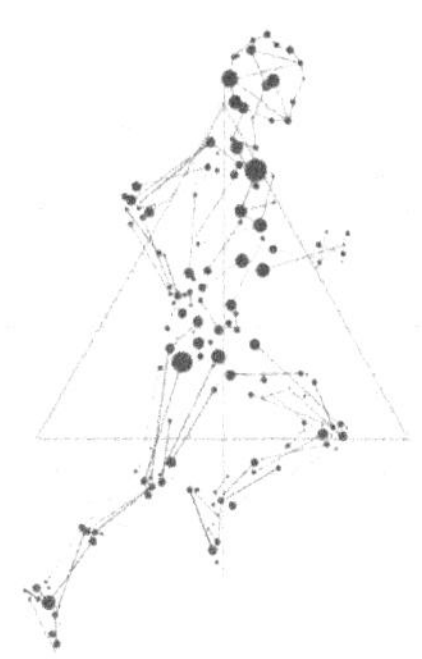

2
Defining Potential

Confucius (Chinese Philosophy): Confucius (c.551–c.479 BC*) believed in the cultivation of wisdom through experience, moral understanding and self-reflection, rather than innate intelligence.*[12]

In the early 1920s, Lewis Terman embodied the very essence of academia. Round spectacles perched on his nose, hair slicked and neatly parted, typically with an expression of deep concentration, Terman was an American psychologist and professor at Stanford University, California.

He was determined, perhaps even consumed, by the idea of proving that IQ (intelligence quotient) stood as the paramount determinant of success in life. This wasn't just a hypothesis for Terman, it was a doctrine, a belief that he pursued.

IQ, of course, refers to a person's logical and reasoning ability. It examines a range of cognitive abilities, including logical reasoning, mathematical ability, spatial recognition, visualization (including being able to manipulate shapes and spaces), language skills, memory and general problem-solving ability.

[12] 'Confucius', *Stanford Encyclopaedia of Philosophy* (first published 31 March 2020). Available from https://plato.stanford.edu/entries/confucius/

Terman embarked on a landmark study in the 1920s called 'The Genetic Studies of Genius'.[13]

Spanning several decades, the study involved c.250,000 school children in California, identifying students with IQs higher than 140 (considered genius level). The average IQ level is 100. A sample of 1,528 students (856 males and 672 females) was selected for the study, with an impressive average IQ of 151. These were students in possession of remarkable gifts in maths, music and literacy, typically displayed from an early age.

These students underwent extensive monitoring of their physical, social, moral and emotional development. The data collected included quantitative measures such as general health, height and weight, as well as qualitative information gathered from interviews with the subjects, their siblings and parents. The study, which began in 1921, aimed to determine the level of success these high-IQ individuals would achieve throughout their lives.

At the heart of this journey was Terman's hypothesis: a belief, steadfast and unyielding, that IQ was the linchpin of objective success; for example, money, notoriety or perhaps even the receipt of Nobel laureate awards.

As the pages of time turned, however, a different truth emerged... a truth that whispered of complexities and subtleties far beyond the crisp precision of an IQ score. In short, Terman was wrong.

In this chapter we explore the myth around IQ and ask an important question: if IQ isn't a key determinant of objective success in life, what is?

The myth

We've come to realize that 'smart' is a spectrum of many shades. This notion intrigues me deeply, especially as someone who, in their final school year, faced teachers' scepticism about my intellectual fitness for purpose. Often, we're our own harshest critics, echoing inner doubts of adequacy.

Yet, this is often a narrative we pen ourselves. A tale of limitations, consisting more of fiction than of fact. In truth, it's not high intelligence or extreme

---

[13] Original publication: L. Terman, *Genetic Studies of Genius* (1926).

talent that script our success stories, but something more nuanced. And often overlooked.

In his captivating book, *Outliers*, Malcolm Gladwell draws an intriguing parallel between IQ and the height requirement in basketball.[14] To pursue a professional basketball career, typically players need to be taller than 6 feet 2 inches. Once a player surpasses a certain height, however, namely 6 feet 6 inches, advantages such as agility, speed and ball-handling start to diminish.

Things get more interesting, however, when we consider how a shorter person can be successful at the sport. Tyrone Curtis 'Muggsy' Bogues stood at only 5 feet 3 inches but played 14 seasons in the National Basketball Association (NBA). Another example is Anthony 'Spud' Webb, who, at 5 feet 6 inches, enjoyed a successful 13-year NBA career, playing 814 games.

To understand how they achieved such success, we should examine the position they played in basketball – point guard. The point guard position is akin to an extension of the coach on the court, responsible for directing the team and making strategic decisions. They prioritize the team's success over individual achievements. Exceptional ball-handling and positional awareness are essential qualities for the player in this role. They excel at reading the defence, orchestrating plays and ensuring their teammates are in optimal positions. Being tall is not a prerequisite for excelling in this role.

IQ levels function in a similar manner, where other competencies can be equally, if not more, important. If IQ were equivalent to height in basketball, then perhaps other, less concisely measurable life skills can, for the purposes of this discussion, be compared to the ball-handling, positional awareness and on-the-court coaching skills of the point guard role on a basketball team. I like to refer to these more abstract and usually *acquired* skills as 'point guard quotient' (PGQ).

To understand PGQ, perhaps we need to explore why elusive PGQ factors do not get measured. To do this, let's look at who decides what IQ tests should try to measure, and why.

---

[14] M. Gladwell, 'The Trouble with Geniuses Part 1' in *Outliers: The Story of Success*, p. 80 (2008).

In 1905, the French Ministry of Education commissioned French psychologists Alfred Binet and Theodore Simonto to create a method of determining which students couldn't effectively learn from regular classroom instruction so that they could receive remedial work.[15] So, IQ tests were essentially used to identify children who needed individualized help outside of school. Not to measure general intelligence.[16] They were intended to identify gaps in core skills – not core skills that mark out the best from the rest. They still largely perform on the same premise today.

IQ tests are typically designed by psychologists and psychometricians (the science of psychological measurement such as cognitive abilities). The design process involves several steps:

- Development of test items: A panel of experts develops a large sample of potential test items. The number of items created initially is higher than what will be included in the final version of the test.[17]
- Pilot testing: The test, with all its items, is administered to a sample of test-takers along with an already-validated IQ test. This step is crucial for testing the validity of the new test.
- Data analysis: The performance of test-takers (number of correct answers) on the new test is compared with their scores on the validated test. The mean and standard deviation of correct answers are calculated to establish a scoring system.
- Item analysis and selection: The correlation between individual test items is analysed (using a statistic called Cronbach's alpha for internal consistency). Items that, when removed, increase the test's internal consistency are dropped from the test.
- Validity and reliability assessment: It's verified whether the test's scores correlate significantly with the scores of the already-validated

[15] R. Siegler, 'The other Alfred Binet' in *Developmental Psychology*, 28(2), 179–190 (1992).

[16] *Do IQ tests actually measure intelligence?* Discover Magazine. Available from www.discovermagazine.com/ mind/ do-iq-tests-actually-measure-intelligence [accessed March 2024].

[17] *How are IQ tests created?* Free IQ Test. Available from www.free-iqtest.org/ how-are-iq-tests-created/ [accessed March 2024].

test (for validity) and whether the test items have a similar difficulty level and measure the same concept (for reliability).[18]

- Standardization: The test is administered to a representative sample of the population to set the norms.
- Finalization: After these steps, the test is refined into its final version, ensuring it's both valid and reliable.

This all sounds pretty thorough but what background, one might ask, does a psychometrician have?

Commonly, one would obtain a bachelor's degree in psychology, education, statistics or a related field. An advanced degree such as a master's or doctoral degree in psychometrics, educational measurement or psychology is also useful. This advanced education is essential for gaining in-depth knowledge in test theory, statistical analysis and psychological assessment.

The student psychometrician would also gain experience through internships or work in settings such as educational institutions, research organizations or testing companies. These environments allow them to apply and hone their skills in test development and analysis.

Finally, they would, or should, acquire some type of certification as a psychometrician, which often involves passing an examination that assesses knowledge and skills in psychometrics. Like most professional qualifications, they would normally also undergo continuing education to stay on top of the latest research, techniques and ethical standards in the field of psychometrics.

They sound very well qualified. However, there's just one thing. They don't tend to come from the business world or the real-life school of hard knocks. In short, psychometricians come from the world of academia. There's nothing wrong with that in itself, but here's the fundamental thing. When it comes to real-life problem-solving, particularly in the world of business, things become more complicated. The core skills to succeed include innovation, in order to exploit an identified need in the marketplace, and the ability to build and manage teams of people. Skills that range from cultural and gender sensitivity to moral reasoning and the ability to inspire people with the vision

---

[18] *Creating an IQ test*, 123test.com. Available from www.123test.com/ creating-an-iq-test/ [accessed March 2024].

of the enterprise. Another critical and nuanced skill involves the careful balance of realism, which must be present when weighing up the pessimistic and optimistic viewpoints of those surrounding decision-makers.

Many aspects of these skills are outside the purview of IQ tests. For example, innovation involves the need for creativity. Measuring creativity in IQ has been a matter of academic debate for decades.[19] IQ and creative ability have historically been treated as unrelated. This viewpoint has shifted in more recent times with tests such as general fluid intelligence tests.[20] These have focused more on abstract reasoning, problem-solving in unfamiliar contexts and the ability to learn new information.

Fluid intelligence is contrasted with crystallized intelligence, which involves using skills, knowledge and perhaps a creative use of an object. How many different ways is it possible to transform a standard wooden pencil, for example? Take a moment and think about this…

How about using it as a musical instrument such as a drumstick, a plant support stick or a stylus for a tablet touch-screen? Or maybe a less obvious use, such as a time capsule? Hollow out the centre of the pencil, creating a small compartment inside. Place a tiny rolled-up piece of paper with a written message or prediction inside. Seal the ends and bury it or hide it as a time capsule.

The latter example perhaps shows a high level of creativity. In any event, science increasingly recognizes creativity as a trait of key importance, and while the focus moves closer to pinpointing creative aspects of the human personality, they appear to remain largely elusive to testing.

Let's look at a real-life example of creativity in action. The year is 1975. Struggling as an actor since 1969, Sylvester Stallone has all but given up. He's spent several years bouncing around bit parts in low-budget movies and staving off financial issues. This, at one point, meant weeks of homelessness. He moved to Hollywood in the early 1970s. At that time (as it

---

[19] *Finding creativity on IQ tests*, Psychology Today. Available from www.psychologytoday.com/ us/ blog/ beautiful-minds/201107/finding-creativity-iq-tests [accessed March 2024].

[20] P. Kyllonen and K. Harrison, *What Is Fluid Intelligence? Can It Be Improved?* (2016).

still is today) Hollywood, was highly competitive. Only very few actors secure successful acting careers.

Stallone, originally from New York, is very resilient and persistent, but he has some limitations to overcome as an actor. These include a distinctive physical appearance and a speech impediment, which arose from complications during his birth. These traits made it challenging for him to fit the conventional leading man archetype prevalent in Hollywood at this time. He's also unknown and lacks the right industry connections. Stallone has no other choice; he has to do something drastic.

'[Stallone] started to write because he couldn't get what he wanted, so he created himself,' said actor Henry Winkler.[21]

There's a lot to explore in that phrase – 'created himself'. How did he do this? Essentially, he had to invent a role for himself by writing a movie script. But Stallone wasn't considered academic at school. He was a troubled child with a difficult upbringing, which resulted in him attending some 13 schools in 12 years. Writing was not his strong point, but he had been toiling with it for several years.

He then managed to get a job as an usher at a cinema in Los Angeles. This allowed him to watch movies every day, and he took the opportunity to record the dialogue in the movies on an audio tape. Afterwards, he would go home to practise writing by replacing the dialogue with his own.

Now let's break this down.

Stallone had hit a wall in terms of his career and saw that he needed to reinvent or create a new version of himself with new skills. Furthermore, he recognized that by creating a new version of himself, he would find a way around the casting agents and narrow preconceptions of Hollywood.

In effect, this was a form of lateral thinking, which is the ability to solve a problem using a creative approach through reasoning that isn't immediately obvious.[22]

---

[21] T. Zimny, director, *Sly*. Produced by Sean Stuart. Starring Sylvester Stallone. Distributed by Netflix (2023).

[22] For more on lateral thinking, see E. De Bono, *The Use of Lateral Thinking* (1967).

In Stallone's case, there was talent there to develop in the first place, but the skill most interesting in this context is creativity or recreation of oneself. Inspired by the Muhammad Ali vs Chuck Wepner boxing match in March 1975, he wrote the original *Rocky* screenplay in just a few days.

Here's the plot twist that you might not be expecting in Stallone's real-life story. The studios loved the screenplay. But they categorically did not want Stallone in it. And they were willing to go to extraordinary lengths to ensure he wasn't in the movie.

In the end, he turned down an offer of $265,000 to sell the rights and *not* appear in the movie. Stallone refused anything but an offer with him in the title role. The studios finally acknowledged the strength of his will and accepted him in the lead part. The rest is history.

Successful entrepreneurs exhibit a wide range of skills, akin to the breadth of skills needed to play the point guard position in basketball. These skills can be learned and developed, unlike innate ones identified in IQ tests. Take the example of Daymond John, the founder of clothing business FUBU. Daymond began working at the age of ten through a programme for underprivileged kids in Brooklyn, New York.[23] His experience working from an early age helped him develop skills such as persuasion, negotiation, discipline, persistence, integrity, trustworthiness and even a charismatic charm.

Despite facing academic challenges, including dyslexia, similar to other renowned success stories such as billionaire Richard Branson, founder of the global Virgin brand, Daymond leveraged his skills to overcome obstacles and achieve success outside the traditional education structure.

Daymond was ruthlessly persistent and hard-working. In the early days of FUBU he and his business partners had managed to sell $400,000-worth of clothes that didn't exist at a show in Las Vegas. After his being turned down by up to 30 banks, Daymond's mother, believing in her son, took out a second mortgage on her home to provide the capital to produce the clothing.[24] Music

---

[23] D. John, *ArticleBio*. Available from www.articlebio.com/daymond-john [accessed March 2024].

[24] A. Banks, *The rise and fall of FUBU*, The Hundreds. Available from https://thehundreds.com/blogs/content/the-rise-and-fall-of-fubu [accessed 19 March 2024].

acts such as LL Cool J played a significant role in promoting the FUBU brand – famously wearing a FUBU hat in a GAP commercial, which significantly boosted revenue. In the following year, 1998, FUBU reached record sales for the business, grossing $350 million worldwide in sales.[25] This was after many years of Daymond ingratiating himself with acts such as LL Cool J – by effectively becoming one of their roadies on away trips. He describes how band members would toss laundry bags his way and how he would do any menial job to help the band. Ultimately he was developing a valuable rapport and striking a clever balance between business and social nuances.

Finally, on this point, I had an unexpected opportunity to speak with a multi-millionaire Irish businessman on this subject several years ago. He told me of the lengths he and his business partners would go to in order to strike rapport with potential big-tech US customers. His strategy was wide-ranging and included dressing in a similar way, researching the industry terminology they used and ultimately socially assimilating their business approach to connect with them across the boardroom table and get deals done. It's difficult to categorize this 'moxie' and 'hustle' shown by go-getters in the business world, but it's real.

Learned competencies and the importance of role models

Robert Oppenheimer (estimated IQ north of 190), known for his role in leading the Manhattan Project during the Second World War, possessed a remarkable level of PGQ to complement his high IQ. When he first met General Leslie Groves in 1942, who interviewed him for the hugely important role, Oppenheimer left a lasting impression:

> 'At the meeting had seemed to cast a spell' … 'he was always, without seeming effort, aware of and responsive to, everyone in the room and was constantly anticipating unspoken wishes.'[26]

---

[25] J. Rucker, *Here's all you need to know about the history of FUBU*, ONE37$_{PM}$ (5 May 2022). Available from www.one37pm.com/style/the-history-of-fubu

[26] R. Monk, *Inside the Centre: The Life of J. Robert Oppenheimer*, p. 335 (2012).

Despite lacking organizational skills and having past associations with communist causes, Oppenheimer convinced Groves that he was the right person to lead the 150,000-strong team tasked with developing the atomic bomb. His selection surprised many, including senior figures within the project. Groves reported being impressed by Oppenheimer's understanding of the urgency of the situation, his ability to explain complex physics to Groves and also his articulation of the need for a centralized headquarters in New Mexico. He was also wowed by Oppenheimer's obvious charm.

Let's unpack this a little. Other much more qualified candidates did not convey this urgency to the general. Oppenheimer not only understood the urgency but also exhibited it in his captivating pitch. It's clear that he was able to read the room and understand not just what to say but how to say it. He was also able to read the urgency and pressure General Groves was under. He listened carefully to him. He took his time to communicate this in language that the general would understand and also struck an obvious rapport. These are essentially PGQ skills on super-charge.

Acquired PGQ

Although 'acquired PGQ' might sound like a medical condition to be avoided, we pause here to look at how these valuable PGQ skills might be developed.

Oppenheimer grew up in a privileged upper-class family, surrounded by resources and opportunities. His parents nurtured his interests and provided everything he needed to explore his passions. Oppenheimer's upbringing instilled in him a confidence. His family encouraged him to express his interests and they provided the necessary tools and resources.

One defining moment in Oppenheimer's life was the support he received from his family while studying at Cambridge University. During his time there he developed resentment towards his tutor, Patrick Blackett, who happened to excel in laboratory skills, an area where Oppenheimer struggled. Emotionally unstable and depressed, he reportedly coated an apple with cyanide and left it on Blackett's desk. The facts thereafter are vague but it appears that, fortunately, the attempt was discovered. Interestingly, the book *Outliers* perhaps misses or certainly underemphasizes one key aspect regarding Oppenheimer's predicament at this point. Julius Oppenheimer, his father, was a seasoned businessman who ran a successful textile importing business in New York. Robert Oppenheimer's state of mind at the time was described as erratic and peculiar, far from the composed negotiator he later became. It's much more likely that his parents, who were highly invested in his education, not Oppenheimer himself, persuaded the college to show leniency.

This example highlights the importance of family support and shelter in enabling one to overcome difficulties and grow skills, as exemplified by Oppenheimer's journey and later ability to do just the same with authority figures. It was a learned behaviour from key role models in his life, such as his father. In *Outliers*, Malcolm Gladwell perhaps attributes these successful negotiations to Robert Oppenheimer alone, but I think it instead illustrates that, with the right kind of family support and shelter, individuals can fulfil their potential and develop the masterful PGQ skills that matter much more in real-life contexts than IQ.

Stallone came from a broken home, had little family support and limited formal education.[27] He had a very different journey to Oppenheimer. One cannot, of course, draw any definitive general conclusions regarding levels of support from working-class, middle-class or even privileged family support, in terms of an individual's development of PGQ skills. Each family is different. Each individual is different. There are, however, a mix of factors and complexities that cater to the development of these skills, and we'll explore these further in later chapters. I think that it is, however, fair to say that many apparent 'success stories' are driven by a combination of life's necessity and an individual's ability to rise and adapt to challenge. A level of IQ has its part to play, but it by no means defines what an individual is capable of.

Terman's IQ theory

Terman's hypothesis, while groundbreaking, didn't capture the intricate tapestry of human success.

The life narratives of Stallone and Oppenheimer were filled with unexpected variables and defy Terman's blinkered approach. Their respective life journeys, like many others in their chosen disciplines, cannot be summed up in a singular metric.

---

[27] He did attend the University of Miami but dropped out.

While some of Terman's study subjects achieved success and became judges and governors, only 70 earned listings in *American Men of Science*, and three were elected to the National Academy of Sciences. Many were indeed considered failures by Terman, given his high standards and expectations. On analysis of the comprehensive data produced on their accomplishments, one author wrote that, while impressive academically, 'Terman's intellectual elite was not of the same calibre as the true scientific elite of the nation.'[28]

Moreover, Terman's meddling in his subjects' lives, providing recommendation letters and leveraging his influence to secure their admission to university, compromised the integrity of the study. Bias also tainted the initial test selection process as candidates were recommended by schoolteachers, resulting in a predominantly white, middle- to upper-middle-class male cohort. These socio-economic advantages skewed the research, as the subjects were already better positioned for success.

Nonetheless, the study did reveal certain benefits associated with high IQ levels. Children with high IQs displayed social aptitude, better adjustment, academic prowess, above-average height and even longer lifespans. However, crucially, they do not account for the guile and lateral thinking skills of history-makers.

Summary

Lewis Terman, the father of educational psychology, essentially proved that IQ is not the paramount determinant of success in life. IQ tests are a tool for measuring certain intellectual abilities. They do not fully encapsulate the broad concept of being 'smart'. Intelligence is a complex and multidimensional trait that extends beyond what's generally measured in standard IQ tests.

The resourcefulness and guile demonstrated by well-known success stories, from Daymond John to Sylvester Stallone, show the ability to view problems from different perspectives.

The power of role-modelling can also be crucial.

---

[28] D. Simonton, *Greatness: Who Makes History and Why* (1994).

Ultimately, the message is that we cannot sum a person up by one IQ test or another. Underestimate yourself and others at your peril. Connect instead with the right intrinsic motivation, support group and opportunities.

And be prepared to surprise yourself!

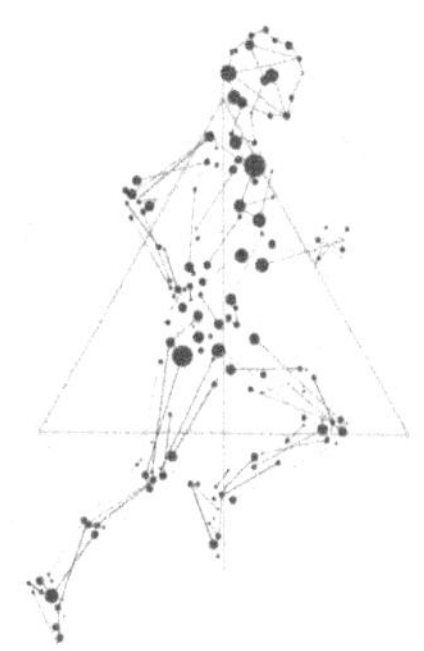

3 The Cornerstone of Decision-Making

Reader's Note: This chapter contains detailed discussions about Adolf Hitler and Joseph Stalin, both of whom played significant roles in the events leading to and during the Holocaust. The material presented here is historical and factual, designed to educate and inform readers but it does concern a dark period in our global history. It's not our intention to cause distress, but we acknowledge that the subject matter may be disturbing for some readers, particularly those with personal or familial connections to the events of the Holocaust.

For those who find this material difficult, we want you to know that there are resources available for support. The Holocaust Memorial Museum (www.ushmm.org) not only offers a wealth of historical information but also has resources for survivors and their families. Similarly, the Holocaust Survivors' Friendship Association (www.holocaustlearning.org.uk) offers support to survivors and their families.

If you wish to contribute towards efforts to preserve the memory and lessons of the Holocaust, consider making a donation to the above institutions or other organizations committed to Holocaust education and survivor support, such as the Claims Conference (www.claimscon.org) and the World Jewish Restitution Organization (www.wjro.org.il).

We implore our readers to approach this chapter with the solemn respect it deserves, bearing in mind the immeasurable suffering endured by the victims of the Holocaust. It's our collective responsibility to ensure their stories are heard, their experiences remembered, and their humanity honoured.

'True humility is not thinking less of yourself; it is thinking of yourself less.'

C.S. Lewis [29]

Germany's attack on Russia stands out as a pivotal moment in the Second World War. Hitler was on a quest to expand the German empire, increasing *Lebensraum*, or living space. Another more practical and important prize, however, glittered in Hitler's eyes. Oil, 'black gold', which was the lifeblood of the German war machine. It had become Hitler's main objective to capture the oil-rich southern regions of the Russian Caucasus.

Prior to the initial assault, Hitler had positioned around three million soldiers along the Russian border, a silent, looming threat that, bizarrely, Stalin ignored despite the clear warnings from his advisors. Stalin ignored these warnings on the faith of empty assurances from the German leader. And then?

On 22 June 1941 millions of German soldiers poured across the Russian border, facing little resistance. Estimates suggest that the Soviet military experienced over 600,000 casualties (killed, wounded and captured) in the first week alone of the German invasion.[30] The Russians were initially paralysed by the unexpectedness of the attack and Stalin's reluctance to

[29] C.S. Lewis, *Mere Christianity* (1952).

[30] For more precise figures and a detailed account, see D. Glantz and J. House, *When Titans Clashed: How the Red Army Stopped Hitler* (1995).

believe that the invasion had even happened. Local commanders were hesitant to act without direct orders, fearing reprisals from Moscow. This hesitation contributed to the early successes of the German attack. They swiftly captured several Soviet territories, including parts of Ukraine, Belarus and the Baltic states (Estonia, Latvia and Lithuania). The German military were well-trained, more experienced and had superior equipment compared to the Russian Army. The German Luftwaffe also had air superiority over the region, enabling them to carry out devastating aerial bombardments on Soviet positions and infrastructure.

As the advance progressed, the plan was for the German forces to surround the city of Stalingrad as part of a larger southern offensive. A sudden change of decision by Hitler to instead capture the city would result in the bloodiest and perhaps the most important battle of the 20th century.

It could be argued that the outcome of this battle was a simple matter of who was the most ruthless dictator. The leader who was most willing to browbeat their subordinates and march endless poor souls to their deaths.

In this chapter, we'll explore the surprising and key factor that won the Battle of Stalingrad, one that's the cornerstone of all good decision-making. Humility.

Decision-making

First, a lesson worth remembering – don't ignore the obvious. We make better decisions, particularly under pressure, by actively seeking out and embracing the viewpoints of trusted advisors. It's a process that can unearth truths and highlight gaps in our knowledge that might otherwise remain shadowed in the corners of our understanding.

Challenger

Robert Ebeling lay 'awake all night certain that the Challenger [shuttle] would blow up on the launch pad the next morning'.[31]

[31] K. Weick, 'The Challenger launch decision: Risky technology, culture, and deviance at NASA' in *Administrative Science Quarterly* 42 (2), 395 (June 1997).

The success of the 1986 *Challenger* space shuttle launch was crucial for NASA (National Aeronautics and Space Administration). The mission was supposed to demonstrate the shuttle's reliability and cost-effectiveness, important in justifying the continued spend on the space programme to the US Congress, amid financial pressures.

Additionally, to garner interest from the media and general public, the first non-astronaut was included in the mission, a media initiative that had worked. Christa McAuliffe, billed as 'the first civilian teacher in space', generated significant public interest and TV coverage. Her inclusion was reinvigorating public engagement with the space programme, which had been waning. These factors combined to create a high-stakes environment.

The pressure was on. In January 1986, the month designated for the launch, there had been delay after delay. The shuttle was initially scheduled to launch on 22 January 1986. The launch was first postponed to 23 January, then to the following day, and subsequently to 25 January. Factors for the delays included the knock-on effect of other delayed shuttle landings. Weather conditions and technical issues also had their part to play. It was then further delayed to 27 January.

NASA had an objective to be able to launch two rockets per month, and these delays meant that *Challenger* was the most delayed launch in NASA's history. This was becoming a major embarrassment. Each delay was also costing hundreds of thousands of dollars. Finally, it was set for launch around 9.30am local time, Tuesday, 28 January 1986.

Ebeling and other engineers had been on a crusade to bring a specific risk regarding the launch to the attention of decision-makers. A year earlier, he and two other engineers at the company had been assigned to examine recovered rocket boosters from the launch of the shuttle *Discovery*, in January 1985. They alarmingly concluded that the rubber O-ring seals on the solid rocket boosters had stiffened in the cold weather, allowing the high-pressure gas inside to leak out.[32] These O-rings did not seem to be able to do their job at low temperatures. The temperature at the time of the *Discovery* shuttle launch in January 1985 was around 53°F, or 12°C.

---

[32] S. Kaplan, 'Finally free from guilt over Challenger disaster, an engineer dies in peace' in *The Washington Post* (22 March 2016).

NASA and Ebeling's company, Morton Thiokol, seemed slow to react to the information. Despite memos in July and August to the powers that be internally, little action was taken. These memos could not have been clearer, with the July 1985 one directed to Morton Thiokol vice-president Bob Lund, detailing the ongoing issues with the O-rings, as the shuttle flights had continued in April and June of 1985. The memo summed up the risk of O-ring failure as a potential 'catastrophe of the highest order – loss of human life'. All of this did prompt a NASA review of the issue in August 1985 – but the pace of launches continued and accelerated.

The inadequate action prompted Ebeling to write a memo in October 1985 (a month when two more shuttles were launched) with the infamous subject heading 'Help'. Help… didn't arrive.

On 27 January 1986, Allan McDonald, Morton Thiokol's Director of Space Shuttle Rocket Booster Project, was concerned about a weather report he had received of a cold front moving in. Temperatures were predicted to be as low as 18°F or *minus* 8°C at the start of the launch window the next morning. To put this in perspective, average lows in January are usually around 55°F, or 13.5°C. It was going to be freakishly cold for the launch; for example, 35°F colder than the launch of the *Discovery* shuttle in January 1985. Knowing the risks that his engineers had made him aware of regarding the O-rings, McDonald called a meeting with NASA officials at 8pm local time that evening. It was going to be a three-way conference call.

What happened next fits squarely into the focus of this chapter's discussion. Robert Ebeling wasn't on the call, but McDonald's engineers comprehensively explained the risks and said they couldn't recommend a launch at temperatures below 53°F, or around 12°C. NASA's rocket launch manager, Lawrence Mulloy, responded by saying, 'When the hell do you want me to launch, next April?' McDonald, who was on the call, was shocked and recalled that this statement was 'very intimidating, to me and everyone else'.[33] This is important. NASA's response was not one of curiosity but rather of confrontation. George Hardy, NASA's deputy director, reportedly added that he was 'appalled' at this recommendation not to launch. Appalled?

---

[33] See Emmy Award-winning documentary about flight STS-51-L and lead-up to the *Challenger* disaster. J. Payne, *Challenger: A Rush to Launch* (2016).

Let's remember that no one expected arctic temperatures such as these in Florida. The engineers were responding to a unique situation with data they had been presenting over and over again for the last six months. It's worth noting that this was the first time in NASA's history that a NASA supplier/contractor had officially opposed a launch. This was not being done lightly. NASA's reaction was unexpected, and the Morton Thiokol engineers were shocked. Knowing the process, however, Hardy then said that he wouldn't go against the contractors' recommendation.

The call was adjourned for a while after McDonald's boss, Bob Lund, said he wanted to discuss the matter off-line with the engineers. McDonald recounts in the Emmy Award-winning documentary on the subject that he found out later what happened in off-line conversations.[34] The 'engineers got put into a position to prove that [the O-rings] would fail at the expected temperatures'. Prove they would fail? Let's take a moment here.

All the engineers were saying was that they didn't have data on how the O-rings would perform below 53°F. They presented evidence showing that even at that temperature the *Discovery* shuttle O-rings 12 months earlier showed evidence of being compromised. It was also an odd way to look at things. For instance, there's a principle applied in environmental and public health contexts to prevent harm to the public. It's termed the 'precautionary principle'.[35] The essence of the test centres on the burden of proof: instead of needing to prove something is a dangerous situation, the principle instead dictates the need to show that it's safe. An approach NASA appeared to depart from.

Finally, an engineer present, Roger Boisjoly, became visibly upset and laid out photographs of the jet-black soot found between the O-rings after one of the earlier flights, clearly in his mind demonstrating the damage direotly related to low temperatures. His words sum it all up: 'Look carefully at these photographs, don't ignore what they are telling you.'[36]

---

[34] J. Payne, *Challenger: A Rush to Launch* (2016).

[35] Its formal articulation is often traced back to German environmental policy in the 1970s, known as *Vorsorgeprinzip*, which means 'precautionary principle' in German.

[36] See Chapter 8: J. McDonald and J. Hansen, *Truth, Lies, and O-rings: Inside the Space Shuttle Challenger Disaster* (2009).

When the call resumed, Lund returned and said they had reassessed the data and that 'it was okay to proceed with the launch as planned'. NASA asked for that in writing. McDonald, not convinced by anything he had heard, was not of a mind to sign a letter to that effect. Matters were taken out of his hands. His boss signed. The launch went ahead, and 73 seconds into the launch the O-rings leaked gas and the rockets exploded, sadly resulting in the deaths of all those on board.

Parallels

I know I'm on dangerous ground here, comparing Stalinist Russia to NASA, one of the most forward-thinking and lauded organizations in the world. But that's the point. The same poor decision-making process can happen anywhere. That same thing is the fact that NASA, it seems, simply didn't have the head space to hear bad news. Stalin had an intolerance for critical feedback and dissenting opinions, which led to a climate of fear and self-censorship in which individuals were often afraid to express their views openly.

By contrast, of course, NASA had a bottom-up, open approach to information that sometimes, though, led to information overload for the decision-makers at the top. They may both, however, have suffered from a phenomenon where a person or organization is unable or unwilling to accept information that suggests a need for significant change or action, due to the cost or difficulty of the required changes. This is sometimes referred to as 'wilful blindness'.[37]

In the context of organizations, this term describes a situation where decision-makers choose to remain ignorant of facts that would necessitate costly or challenging corrections, thereby avoiding the need to address potentially significant issues.

Stalin didn't have the head space to deal with the fact that Hitler was about to double-cross him and attack his country. He clung irrationally to the

[37] For more on this physiological concept, see the work of Margaret Heffernan. Her Marginalian website delves into the psychology of wilful blindness, exploring how individuals and organizations often choose not to see or acknowledge obvious truths or facts. Available from www.themarginalian.org/2014/08/27/willful-blindness-margaret-heffernan/

non-aggression pact the two had signed in 1939 and also to the fact that he couldn't understand Hitler's logic of opening a second front, a war in the east as well as the west.

Hitler vs Stalin

In many ways Hitler and Stalin were very similar. They both rank around the top of history's most brutal dictators, particularly in terms of sheer mass murder. They were both completely devoid of any compassion, obsessed with their own skewed ideologies and they absolutely ruled with an iron fist. The decision-making process that both fostered was characterized by authoritarianism, centralization of power and a lack of dissent. They sought to maintain tight control over decision-making processes and expected unwavering obedience from their subordinates. There was, however, one important difference in the culture of decision-making that each fostered around them. Hitler and Stalin both valued loyalty in their inner circles, but Hitler placed a greater emphasis on loyalty than competency. He tended to have a small group of trusted advisors, such as Hermann Göring, Heinrich Himmler and Joseph Goebbels, who each held influential positions within the Nazi regime. These individuals, however, were primarily responsible for implementing Hitler's directives rather than offering critical feedback or challenging his decisions. They were loyalists who shared his ideology, creating an echo chamber that limited the diversity of perspectives.

When the surprise invasion of Russia occurred, Stalin recognized that he had made a colossal error of judgement regarding Hitler. His first reaction was disbelief, then he flew into a rage, muttering, 'Everything is lost, I give up. Lenin left us a great legacy, but we, his heirs, have ****ed it up.'[38] He disappeared from public view, a broken man, devoid of confidence in his decision-making abilities. When his generals entered his residence around a week later, a dishevelled Stalin was found sitting in a chair staring into space. He'd had an emotional breakdown and assumed that his generals had come to arrest him for his incompetence. When he learned that they wanted him

---

[38] R. Freemann, Jr, 'Operation Barbarossa: How Stalin was blindsided by Berlin: Soviet leader Joseph Stalin refused to believe that his country was about to be invaded by Nazi Germany – until it happened with Operation Barbarossa' in *War History Network* (Spring 2018).

to return to Moscow to lead them, it gave him a second chance, one that he hadn't expected.

Humility

Stalin returned to the Kremlin with a mindset shifting from despair to enlightened self-interest. He was suddenly prepared to acknowledge that he didn't have all the answers. Seeing perhaps for the first time that he needed the input and decision-making capacity of others to save his own skin.

First, he made a radio speech to the country. He frankly admitted that most of the western Soviet Union had been lost to the German forces. He spoke to his people as 'brothers and sisters, and dear friends'. He then appointed competent military leaders and delegated more authority to them. He recognized the need for experienced commanders and, learning from his past mistakes, he allowed them greater decision-making power. Figures such as Georgy Zhukov, Konstantin Rokossovsky and Aleksandr Vasilevsky emerged as capable field commanders. Stalin relied on their expertise in planning and executing military operations.

He also established front commands (regional military headquarters) to oversee operations in different areas of the Soviet Union. This decentralized structure allowed for more effective coordination and delegation of authority. Front commanders had more autonomy in managing their operations and coordinating with subordinate units, contributing to improved decision-making and flexibility on the battlefield.

Modern-day behavioural science has begun to recognize the importance of this sort of humility in decision-making. Researchers led by Dr Mark Leary, a professor of psychology and neuroscience at Duke University, pioneered the development of an intellectual humility scale to assess among other things the openness we might possess to consider the views of others when making decisions. The scale consists of different levels.[39]

---

[39] The Intellectual Humility Scale (IHS) was developed by a team of researchers led by Mark Leary at Duke University. The scale was introduced in their paper titled 'The nature, motives, and consequences of intellectual humility', published in the *Journal of Personality and Social Psychology* in 2017.

Higher scores on the scale reflect greater levels of intellectual humility. Stalin's intellectual humility had perhaps increased dramatically as a result of his obvious decision-making shortcomings.

Hitler, on the other hand, was intoxicated by a megalomaniac vision and simply saw any decision he made as infallible. It was now his turn to make a huge mistake. Following his successful Blitzkrieg tactics, which began with him rolling his tanks into Poland in 1939, subsequent victories were rapid, occupying Norway, Denmark, Belgium and the Netherlands by 1940. The most striking success came with the fall of France in June 1940, when German forces steamrolled French troops, leading to the French surrender and the occupation of Paris within weeks of entering the country. Hitler incorrectly assumed the same would happen in Russia, hence his famous quote: 'All we've got to do is kick the door in and the whole edifice will come crumbling down.'[40]

He was so overconfident that he made most of the key decisions with information over the telephone from a base over 1,400km away from the front lines in his centralized HQ in modern-day Poland. As the Battle of Stalingrad began, General Paulus, in command of the German 6th Army, became increasingly disillusioned with Hitler. Hitler had refused to allow a strategic retreat from the city following failure to make progress. Paulus recognized the dire situation his army was in, trapped and surrounded by Soviet forces, and he reportedly requested permission to break out of the encirclement rather than continue to fight in a hopeless situation. Hitler, who expected Paulus to fight to the last man, denied his request to retreat.

Failure to accept information from people closest to it on the ground? This sounds familiar. Again, we refer to the NASA example, which couldn't be more different in terms of ideology and endless other metrics, but this makes it all the more surprising and insightful. Disclaimer: this is a comment on the human condition only. NASA was overconfident. Risk-taking, particularly in 1985, had begun to become normalized. In a comprehensive review of the culture at NASA during that period, Diane Vaughen, American Sociologist at Columbia University, concluded: 'In 1985 there was both an escalating concern about safety and belief that risk was acceptable.'

---

[40] For an account of Hitler's attitudes and statements regarding the invasion of the Soviet Union, refer to works such as: R. Evans, *The Third Reich at War* (2009).

There had been nine shuttle launches in nine months leading up to the *Challenger* disaster in January 1986. Their target was to double that number. Morton Thiokol Inc., the company Allan McDonald worked for, was on the verge of concluding a large new order of some 65 rockets. So they were under pressure to please their main customer, NASA. In one final telling note, McDonald recalls, after the teleconference resumed on the evening of Monday, 27 January 1986, the night before the launch: 'No one from NASA had any questions about the validity of the data used to change the recommendation from don't launch to launch.'[41]

It's worth dwelling on this; NASA didn't challenge any of the data when the call resumed. McDonald goes on to make the vital point that NASA had challenged all the data the engineers had originally presented that had opposed the launch, before the break in the call. Of course, things had always worked out before.

General Paulus ultimately surrendered the 6th Army in February 1943, marking a significant defeat for Germany and a turning point in the Second World War.

Summary

We should all do well to retain humility, regardless of past successes. Shutting out the views of others, particularly trusted advisors presenting obvious, data-driven information, can be catastrophic.

---

[41] See Chapter 8: J. McDonald and J. Hansen, *Truth, Lies, and O-rings: Inside the Space Shuttle Challenger Disaster* (2009).

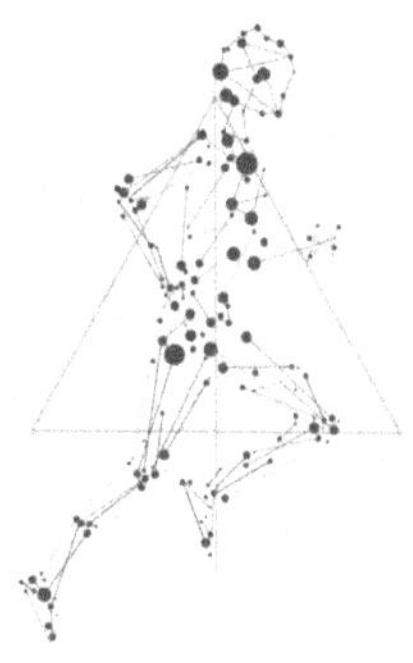

4

Atomic Motivation

'Wu Wei', or effortless action, aligns with doing things for their own sake and finding joy in the action itself – Lao Tzu's teachings.[42]

At Yale University in the early 1960s, a participant, a regular individual drawn from everyday life, stepped into an unfamiliar environment. This individual was here for an experiment, the full extent of which remained a mystery. Each of the participants was greeted by an officious-looking professor wearing a tie, lab coat and holding a clipboard. The professor embodied the authority and professional rigour of the academic setting. Their presence commanded a certain gravitas, an unspoken expectation of respect.

The participants were introduced to the experiment's purpose: a study of learning and memory. The objective was to assess the potential role of punishment in improving the memory retention of the subjects. Our participant was instructed to teach word pairs to a 'learner', another participant.

Unknown to each other, for every mistake the learner made, the 'teacher' (participant) had to administer an electric shock, which increased in intensity

[42] See Laozi and H-G Moeller. *Daodejing: The New, Highly Readable Translation of the Life-Changing Ancient Scripture Formerly Known as the Tao Te Ching* (2015).

with each error. The switches before them were labelled with voltages, escalating from a mild shock to levels marked as dangerous. Unknown to the 'teacher' administering the shocks, the lab-coated professors and the would-be subjects receiving those electric shocks were merely actors.

The purpose of the experiment was a lie. This wasn't a memory test but rather a ruse to see whether people, when directed by an authority figure, would do unusual, dangerous or sometimes downright evil things.

The memory of the atrocities committed during the Holocaust was fresh in the minds of those designing the experiment. This experiment's findings would later be published by Stanley Milgram and entitled 'Behavioural study of obedience experiment', referred to as 'the Milgram experiments'.[43] The experiments would become famous in social psychology history for the demonstration of 'obedience'. Astonishingly, 65% of the total number of participants ultimately went on to administer what they thought to be fatally dangerous levels of electricity to a complete stranger. Just because they were told to do it by an authority figure. This is a fact made all the more incredible when we consider the efforts made by the actors (hidden from view) supposedly receiving these shocks. Despite the screams of pain and begging from these actors, the teacher-participants continued administering the shocks, usually after some dialogue with their overseeing lab-coated professor.

The results, dramatic as they were, did not necessarily demonstrate obedience. Other key factors were at play, which remained overlooked for many years, factors that are insightful and fundamental to understanding motivation.

In this chapter, we'll explore how people can be motivated to do extraordinary things and perhaps equally, if not more importantly, how we can use this knowledge to persuade and motivate ourselves.

The nature of motivation

To start, let's examine what motivates us into action. Behavioural science tells us that there are two primary types of motivation stimuli: intrinsic and extrinsic factors, each with distinct characteristics that impact on our behaviour.

---

[43] S. Milgram, 'Behavioural study of obedience' in *Journal of Abnormal and Social Psychology* 67 (4), 371–378 (1963).

Intrinsic motivation emerges from within. It's driven, for example, by an individual's personal interests, curiosity or desire for mastery. A musician who practises daily out of love for music or a writer driven by a passion for storytelling is intrinsically motivated. Intrinsic motivation often involves phrases such as 'I love doing this', 'this is really interesting' or 'I enjoy learning about this'. Their actions are fuelled by internal satisfaction and a sense of personal accomplishment.

In contrast, extrinsic motivation is influenced by external factors; to earn a reward or avoid punishment. A student studying hard to get good grades or an employee working overtime for a bonus exemplifies extrinsic motivation, frequently marked by statements such as 'I need to do this to get that', or 'if I do this, I'll be rewarded with that'. The key distinguishing factor is that the focus is on the reward at the end, not the activity itself. To understand this at a deeper level let's look at an example.

Mardy Fish

As a personality, Mardy Fish was an easy-going 'surfer dude' type of tennis player, who usually wore beads and an easy smile. Mardy was never a tennis prodigy, but he was good enough to be selected for an elite tennis training academy at Saddlebrook, Florida. The fact that his father was a former tennis pro and coach had its part to play. Saddlebrook was the premier centre of excellence for US tennis players in the 1990s. Fast forward to 2008, Mardy was ranked number 123 in the world – which was good but not what he had hoped for in his tennis career.

Turning 28 years old, an age at which many tennis players consider retirement, he reflected on his career. He realized that he hadn't got everything out of it that he could have, or that he believed he *should* have. Mardy desperately wanted to make sure that when he was done playing, he would know that he had tried everything he possibly could to get the best out of himself. He concluded that he would never be at peace if he didn't give it everything and truly see what he was capable of. So, at the end of the 2008 season, he established a series of goals, including losing weight and reaching peak physical fitness. He reorganized his training team and began to work as hard as he could. All day, every day.

He stopped drinking alcohol and went on a strict athlete's diet. He started to get more sleep, sometimes going to bed as early as 7.30pm. He stopped seeing friends. He was obsessed; every decision in his life involved tennis. The fitter he became, the longer he trained. He slept in a hyperbaric oxygen chamber to speed up recovery from training. In two and half months he lost 31lbs in weight.

Let's reflect on this for a moment, as there's a lot to consider. This is someone who's completely devoted to this one goal. This is not normal behaviour. He has stopped seeing friends and tennis has taken over his life – to the extent that he later works himself to the point of illness, another issue we'll explore later. Where does that come from? Well, we're about to get some clues. At the start of the 2009 season he was ready to see results.

He began the tennis season at a lesser-known tournament in New England, reaching the quarter-finals, where he faced a buddy of his called Frank Damselfish. He didn't play well, quickly losing the first set. At that moment something snapped in him. Bizarrely, he could be seen slapping himself on the face on the tennis court, as he reached an internal crisis point. Seemingly out of nowhere, he shouted to Damselfish, 'You're not going to beat me! You're never going to beat me, I'm fxxking coming back to win!' The umpire and Damselfish were in shock. This aggression was completely out of character for the mellow player they had known. It was enough to knock Damselfish off his stride. Mardy played like a demon from then on, won the game and went on to win the tournament and $75,000 in prize money. He later commented that this outburst came from some part of his mind that he didn't know was there. He had lost a friend but transformed his game.

Let's look more closely at this. Mardy had made this huge physical effort. He had sacrificed so much and had seen the results in training. Playing poorly was not what he expected in terms of his return to tournament tennis. He seems surprised by the sudden emergence of this anger that essentially drove him on to win. I happen to have personal experience of this type of self-directed anger. It was one of the key motivators driving me to work extremely hard over a period of years to ultimately qualify as a solicitor, from a low-base 'standing start' during my school days. I experienced this as a burning need to take action, doing extreme things like regularly getting up at 5.30am or 6am to study before school. Essentially, doing whatever it took to attack the challenge, with everything I had.

Neuroscience tells us that anger, like other emotions, comes from the limbic system in our brains. This is a complex network nestled deep in our brain, which acts almost like a highly intuitive and responsive social media feed, constantly reacting to the stimuli around us. When we experience changes in our external environment, our limbic system processes these sensory emotional cues. It's a blunt instrument designed to guide and stimulate us to react. The information is transmitted to the prefrontal cortex part of our brains, which in turn decides how to act on these emotions.

In a stressful or threatening environment, the limbic system kicks into high gear. In Mardy's case the fight response was perhaps triggered and it engaged the powerful emotion of anger. This can be destructive and negative, but when harnessed can also be powerful short-term fuel for motivation.[a]

Intrinsic motivation in this context is akin to atomic energy. It's a fusion of our core values and deep-rooted interests when exposed to events that may challenge these. The energy produced can be immense and long-lasting. In contrast, extrinsic motivation, while effective in the short term, often leads to dependency on external rewards. Reliance on these external rewards may burn bright in terms of motivation, for a short time; however, they have downsides. When these rewards are taken away, motivation diminishes over time.[44]

There are of course big extrinsic rewards in tennis, such as the prestige and acclaim of being US number one, or all those cash prizes, but I don't think that was it. For example, in the documentary about his life by Netflix (*Breaking Point*), Mardy refers to the assumption everyone seemed to have made about him, particularly in the media.[45] Essentially, he had already done everything he was capable of doing by the end of the 2008 season. Proving people wrong is a very powerful extrinsic motivator – to kick-start our actions. There are, however, only so many times you can prove people wrong and so many times you can say I told you so.

Researching Mardy's career and motivation, you get the sense that there's something deeper at play. He uses the sentence in the documentary: 'I desperately wanted to make sure that when I was done playing, I could put

---

[44] G. Loewenstein, 'The psychology of curiosity: A review and reinterpretation' in *Psychological Bulletin* 116 (1), 75–98 (1994).

[45] C. Way and M. Way, directors, *Untold: Breaking Point* (2021).

my head on my pillow every night, knowing that I tried everything I could possibly do.' The key phrase here is 'put my head on my pillow'. Even taking into account external achievement and validation, the dominant force was something else. It was a deep intrinsic motivation characterized by engaging in an activity for personal satisfaction and the fulfilment it brings. In essence, Mardy tapped into a need to prove to himself he was capable of applying the effort, to get the best out of himself. The outcome sought was the satisfaction of knowing that he gave it everything. Ultimately, he wanted peace of mind, a deep-seated intrinsic motivation that became the 'power cell' of meaningful change.

From there, Mardy Fish's career trajectory took a remarkable turn, soaring from 123rd to 7th in the world rankings within two years. He found an extra gear, pushing himself to unprecedented levels of effort and, ultimately, astonishing outcomes.

Motivation – rediscovery

We sometimes look at motivation back to front. We assume there must be an outcome or reward in order to get us or others motivated to act. This is not what science shows us. One of the key experiments demonstrating the natural motivation of primates to solve problems, particularly in relation to extrinsic motivation, was conducted by Harry F. Harlow in 1949. In his experiment, Harlow presented eight rhesus monkeys with a mechanical problem-solving task, involving pulling out a vertical pin, undoing a hook and unhinging a cover. Remarkably, without any external incentives such as food or water, or any specific instructions, the monkeys not only engaged with the task but also performed exceptionally well. All eight monkeys completed the challenge within two weeks, and two-thirds did so in under 60 seconds.

Intrigued by these results, Harlow's team introduced an external motivator in a second trial, offering raisins as a reward for successful completion of the task. Contrary to expectations, this extrinsic motivation did not enhance performance. Instead, it resulted in more errors and less frequent problem-solving by the monkeys. Rather than aiding their performance, the food reward seemed to become a distraction.

These findings were pivotal in shifting the understanding of motivation. Previously, motivation was largely understood in terms of biological needs (such as hunger or thirst) and external rewards or punishments. Harlow's experiment, however, indicated that neither biological needs nor external rewards were the primary drivers of the monkeys' behaviour. This led Harlow to propose a new theory of human behaviour centred on intrinsic reward. He suggested that the motivation for problem-solving was organically derived from an inherent interest in the task itself, independent of biological needs or external incentives.[46] In many ways this can simply be understood and observed by watching any toddler play and learn. We all have a natural motivation fuelled by the activity that we're interested in. Understanding this reframes the challenge. It's not to become motivated, it's to avoid becoming demotivated.

Psychologists Edward L. Deci and Richard M. Ryan have extensively researched this topic. Their self-determination theory emphasizes the importance of intrinsic motivation and its role in fostering autonomy.[47] Both intrinsic and extrinsic motivations are important, it seems; however, intrinsic motivation often leads to deeper, more enduring effort and effectiveness.

As mentors, coaches and parents, the learning here is that there's a natural motivation among those we guide. Our job perhaps becomes more about empowerment, creating space and avoiding demotivation. For Mardy this space to rediscover his mojo for tennis was helped in no small part by the three Ts. In Daniel Pink's fascinating book, *Drive*, the theory of motivation particularly focuses on the three Ts: time, task and team, and is a revolutionary approach in understanding what drives us in the workplace.[48] Pink argues that when individuals have control over their time, they can work when they feel most productive and creative. Control over task allows people to engage in work that they find meaningful and challenging, fostering a sense of purpose and mastery. Finally, having a say in choosing their team empowers individuals to collaborate with those who inspire and complement their skills. This autonomy in the three Ts creates an environment where motivation can thrive, leading to higher satisfaction and productivity.

---

[46] T. Theodore, 'Harlow monkey experiment (definition + contribution to psychology)' in *Practical Psychology* (16 February 2022).

[47] R. Ryan and E. Deci, 'Self-Determination Theory and the Facilitation of Intrinsic Motivation, Social Development, and Well-Being' in *American Psychologist* 55, 68–78 (2000).

[48] D. Pink, *Drive: The Surprising Truth About What Motivates Us* (2009).

Mardy Fish at this point in his career had control of these key elements, which allowed him to focus on a rediscovery of the intrinsic elements of training and playing. Tennis is a game that offers a blend of physical and mental challenges, requiring agility, strength, strategy and concentration. The satisfaction of mastering difficult shots or outmanoeuvring an opponent provides a strong sense of accomplishment in itself. There's such an important lesson for us all here in terms of how we can rediscover our own motivation in the things we love doing by recognizing and creating the space necessary.

Persuasion

Returning to our introductory story, the Milgram experiments initially seemed to suggest a simple obedience to authority, but further analysis by researchers such as Haslam and Reicher suggests a more complex interplay of factors.[49] Gradual persuasion, through the mechanism of incremental increases in shock voltage, played a significant role in the participants' decision-making. The fact of the matter was that when participants checked in with their lab-coated overseers, they were simply read a list of standard responses.

Ultimately, participants tended to go along with the experiment if the response to their queries justified their actions in terms of the scientific benefits of the study and, in turn, wider society. Linking their actions to a wider purpose was powerful. Responses such as 'the experiment requires that you continue' were effective. However, if given a direct order such as 'you have no other choice, you must go on', participants typically refused and ended the experiment. In addition, the power of the incremental ratcheting up was hugely significant. The deeper the participants got in, the harder it was to stop.

There's a final interesting learning here. Gradual persuasion is a power tool often used by con artists or cultural corruption, as we'll explore later. We can use this in a positive way, however, by kick-starting positive actions with small steps.[50] The next time you plan to take a run, for instance, don't think about

---

[49] S. Haslam and S. Reicher, 'Contesting the "nature" of conformity: What Milgram and Zimbardo's studies really show' in *PLOS Biology* (20 November 2012).

[50] For more in this area, see M. Konnikova, *The Confidence Game* (2016).

the rain outside or how you're feeling at that moment. Instead, ratchet up the persuasion. Postpone judgement on whether you'll take that run or not. Instead, focus on getting your running shoes and gear ready (preferably the night before). Put them on and wear them around the house. Then maybe stand outside. Perhaps do a warm-up. If you don't feel like a run then stop, guilt-free, and try again tomorrow. You may just be surprised at how effective these 15-volt increments of motivation can be.

Summary

The Milgram experiments identify an initially hidden insight into human behaviour. The ability to persuade people with low intrinsic motivation, using graduated actions and banked momentum. This insight is truly valuable when applied particularly in the context of persuading ourselves to do positive but difficult things.

Extrinsic rewards in life tend to be short-lived in duration but are enough to be a useful tool in kick-starting us into action. They come with the health warning of potentially impeding intrinsic motivation if used incorrectly. For powerful long-term motivation, intrinsic motivators are much more potent. They tap into our inherent tendency to seek out novelty and challenge in an organic, natural way. White-hot burning motivation typically comes from a place of deep personal meaning. A place where the pursuit of the goal becomes intertwined with self-worth, identity or seeking fundamental needs such as contentment, for example in the knowledge that you gave an opportunity everything you had.

Rediscovering and sustaining motivation then becomes more about avoiding demotivation. Nurturing that delicate flame with the autonomy and space needed to grow, both in ourselves and those we mentor. Following this path, we can truly tap into something atomic.

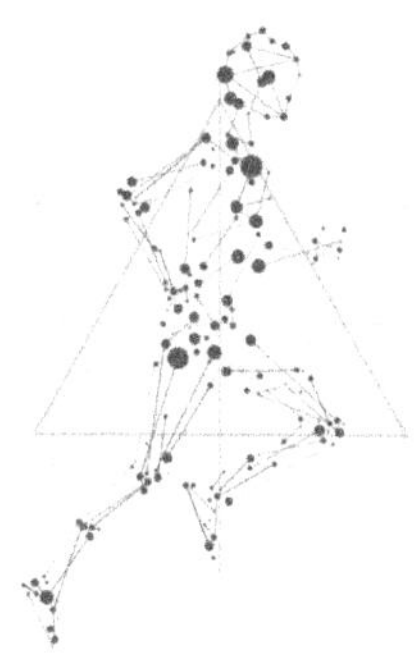

5 Mastery

'What disturbs minds is not events but our judgements on events.'[51]
Epictetus Greek Stoic philosopher (c. AD 50–135)

Confucianism (China): Confucius emphasized the importance of continuous learning and self-improvement. He believed that mastery comes through dedication and the relentless pursuit of knowledge. His quote, it 'does not matter how slowly you go as long as you do not stop', highlights the significance of perseverance on the path to mastery.[52]

Matti Nykänen was one of the greatest ski jumpers that ever lived. The Flying Finn, as he was dubbed, soared to an unprecedented Olympic glory, winning four gold medals, three of them at the 1988 Winter Olympics in Calgary, Canada.

With the audacity of an 18-year-old, he clinched his first World Championship gold medal in 1982, and a staggering five World Championship gold medals by 1989. Nykänen was known for his aggressive and fearless approach to

[51] Epictetus. *Enchiridion.* Translated by George Long (2004).

[52] *The life and wisdom of Confucius*, Ultra Unlimited. Available from www.ultra-unlimited.com/blog/the-life-and-wisdom-of-confucius-chinas-great-sage-who-guided-humanity-toward-goodness [accessed 2024].

jumping. He was willing to take risks and push the limits, which often resulted in extraordinary performances. It was a career that didn't just make him a sporting superstar, it catapulted him into the echelons of mythic athletes.

In the cinematic world, Nykänen's fictional encounter with British ski jumping contender Michael Edwards in *Eddie the Eagle* serves as an intriguing point of departure for our exploration into the subject of mastery.

While this particular encounter at the 1988 Olympics never transpired in reality, due to Nykänen's limited English proficiency, the creative licence taken by the film offers a compelling segue into this subject. The film portrays Nykänen remarking to Edwards that they're more similar than anyone else in the competition. Not necessarily in the delivery of their performance, but rather in the 'why' of their pursuit.

Edwards, the first British ski jumper to brave the event since 1928, faced the disdain of the British skiing establishment, and ultimately finished last in the ski jump competition. But it was his ability to try against all the odds that endeared him to the Olympic fan base and further afield. His open self-deprecation was refreshing in such a precise and pressurized sport. He even once termed himself 'Eddie the Ostrich' as opposed to an eagle!

However, it was not for victory in the conventional sense that Edwards took daring leaps off those towering slopes. Nykänen, rather, sums up their similarity as competitors as doing it to 'free our souls'. It's the thirst for personal growth and the pure love of the sport that drives champions like him to greatness. In the crucible of competition, it's the 'why' that kindles the fires of excellence, pushing athletes to reach unparalleled heights, irrespective of winning trophies and medals.

In earlier chapters of this book, we've delved into the world of tennis and examined some remarkable careers. Tennis serves as a great example of people who, even though they seem to have achieved everything in the sport, continue to dominate. Novak Djokovic, for example, holds the all-time record of 24 major singles titles and at the time of writing is still world number one. He's the only man in history to be the reigning champion of all four majors at once across three different surfaces (2016), and the only one to complete a triple career grand slam (2023).

How do these titans of sport maintain their relentless drive and fierce competitiveness, even after conquering every conceivable title?

A clue, perhaps, is found in the realm of motor racing. A domain often romanticized in cinematic form. The movie *Ford v. Ferrari* depicts Christian Bale's character, the legendary driver Ken Miles, imparting a poignant lesson to his son about the essence of motivation. Miles speaks of the elusive pursuit of the 'perfect lap', an artistry requiring impeccable judgement on braking, acceleration, cornering and optimal angles.

In brief – perfection of an art. It's the quest for mastery to achieve perfection that propels the finest in every discipline. It's the 'why' that ignites their inner fire, compelling them to extract the utmost from themselves each and every time, regardless of the performance of the competition.

This, however, isn't the exclusive terrain of elite performers. It's a mindset that we can all lean towards, from the novice to the Olympian. If we can collectively shift our focus towards the pursuit of flawless execution as the ultimate goal, rather than fixating on outdoing competitors or securing victory in specific competitions, we might discover a hitherto overlooked and profoundly enlightening path in life.

In this chapter, we'll explore just that.

The maths myth

At school, mathematics can be a personal nemesis. It certainly was for me. I wrestled with its complexities for years, just trying to stay afloat in the sea of equations and theorems. It wasn't until I repeated my final year in school that I sought extra help from a teacher from a different school. I filled in the gaps in my fundamental knowledge and managed to perform reasonably well in my repeat final year exams.

Looking back, I realize how fortunate I was to have access to a car at the time, which eased the burden of travelling for extra lessons. Something not every student has.

But my maths struggles are a common thread in conversations with others who believe they're simply not wired for the subject. Meanwhile, there are those students who seem to effortlessly grasp mathematical concepts as if it were second nature. The emphasis on mathematics, especially in university STEM courses (science, technology, engineering and mathematics), is undeniable.

Policymakers and industry leaders are increasingly alarmed by a shortage of STEM professionals, a scarcity seen as critical for sustaining innovation, global competitiveness and even national security.

Salman 'Sal' Amin Khan, the American educator and founder of Khan Academy, sheds light on the conundrum of modern maths education. He questions the effectiveness of our teaching system, which tends to group students by age and perceived ability. The traditional teaching system of course includes lectures on mathematical concepts, assigning homework and the administration of tests.

Even if we take a high-class *average* score of 60% achieved on these tests, this leaves a substantial knowledge gap of 40%. And then what do we do?

We forge ahead. Usually into more advanced subject matter, often built upon the shaky foundation of what we've just learned. If we take a step back we can see that, with this traditional system of learning, what we've set in stone is the learning *period* window, not the *outcome.*

Khan likens this approach to the example of constructing a house. Imagine giving a builder a strict timeframe of a few weeks to complete each floor to the best of their ability. At the end of this period, an inspection might reveal glaring gaps – wet cement, angles slightly askew – representing a construction deficiency of possibly 40%.

But, instead of addressing these gaps, we promptly move on to the next floor, piling complexity upon imperfection. Each floor must be completed within a similar timeframe. It's a matter of virtual certainty that, at some point, there will be a catastrophic failure in the construction, rendering the dwelling unsafe to inhabit. In a parallel fashion, mathematics students may find themselves disengaging from the subject as the curriculum races ahead, leaving them without the foundational knowledge needed to intelligently question the new material and absorb it effectively.

Khan seeks, in a TED Talk, to debunk the common perception that certain subjects are just beyond the grasp of the general public.[53] It is, rather, our traditional system of learning that makes them feel this way. He notes that

---

[53] See S. Khan, *Let's teach for mastery – not test scores.* TED (September 2015). Available from www.ted.com/talks/sal_khan_let_s_teach_for_mastery_not_test_scores

complex subjects such as organic chemistry, for example, are regarded as something only a minority can understand, even with the right traditional learning resources. However, he notes that if we were to embark on a journey in a time machine, transporting ourselves back 400 or 500 years, we could examine literacy levels – a quintessential basic skill of our present time. At that historical juncture, literacy rates may have languished around 15%.

Engaging with someone who could read and write at that time, perhaps a religious cleric, might lead them to estimate that, with proper schooling, society could elevate literacy rates to 30% in the future. Yet, as we know today, levels have ascended to around 86% globally and 95% in most countries for basic literacy. Why?

The answer lies in the fact that literacy is not regarded as a discretionary, optional skill; it's deemed essential. Consequently, we allocate whatever time is necessary to ensure individuals attain mastery, particularly of the fundamentals.

Now, let's ponder the disparity between this and achieving the requisite STEM literacy levels in students. The pivotal distinction rests in the objective. What's fixed, in this approach, is the *timeframe*. Essentially, we're baking in knowledge gaps that are likely to surface later, hindering mastery.

When we seek to elevate literacy rates, we marshal resources, which abound in our digital age – internet resources, remote tutoring, a plethora of educational apps, parental intervention and so on. Meanwhile, we acknowledge that time efficiency is of course a factor.

As such, our metaphorical house construction, for example, must leave a margin of flexibility for the build, allowing time for late deliveries, bad weather and unforeseen events. Crucially, we must refrain from advancing to the next level until each student has constructed a *sufficient* foundation of understanding at the current stage.

It's essentially up to adults, in many respects, to function as role models for the next generation. We must dispense with the perhaps implied conditioning that 'you're not a maths person'. Instead, we must embrace the notion that, with the right allocation of time, approach and teaching, the mastery of nearly anything is within our grasp.

In an ideal world, re-establishing the reason why should melt away counterproductive fixed learning timeframes and refocus instead on the joy of learning.

The fragile world we create for ourselves

There's another flaw that can get baked into our approach. That flaw is one of *tangled* identity. It's apparent that many people think that their self-worth is in some way entangled with their performance in particular situations, such as exams, sports competitions, business outcomes, etc.

While, of course, genetics has its part to play in our ability to do certain things, people (myself included for a time) tend to take failure very personally. This can have a debilitating effect on how we deal with inevitable challenges in our lives.

There's a nuance here to clarify. Taking defeats personally can be a great motivator to work harder, which is great when applied in a healthy way. This is not what we're addressing here. Our focus here is the danger of identifying failure as a personal flaw or innate limitation, thus critically damaging motivation at a key moment.

As our opening quote in this chapter from Epictetus the Greek Stoic philosopher stated, it's our judgement of outcomes that can be flawed and damaging. It's a worthy goal to begin to see outcomes *more* as a product of the amount of work put in and as an opportunity for refinement, focus and growth.

Carol Dweck is Professor of Psychology at Stanford University and specializes in the area of growth mindset. She has conducted thought-provoking research in this area. One of many such studies involved children of around ten years old being given three maths tests. One easy, one difficult and another easy one, in that order. They set the tough test at quite a difficult level and monitored the opinions of the children both before and after the tests. Interestingly, some children loved the idea of challenge and happily uttered phrases such as 'I was hoping this would be informative'.[54]

---

[54] C. Dweck, *Mindset: The New Psychology of Success* (2007).

All the students struggled with the tough test in the middle but found the initial one easy. The third test revealed a very interesting insight. Certain students saw themselves as having a fixed amount of ability. They either had it or they didn't. They were, in their own minds, either smart or dumb. The students who believed they were dumb did very poorly on the third test, which was at the same standard as the first test they had done well in.

What's going on here? It turns out that their confidence was shattered. These students who Dweck categorizes as of 'fixed mindset' felt this was a measure of their intelligence and were devastated by the outcome of the second test. They associated their performance as a measure of self-worth (a powerful emotion as we know from Chapter 1 of this book) and felt entirely dejected.

We have to be careful here. Attributing blanket labels such as 'fixed' and 'growth mindset' to a group of people can be a gross oversimplification given the multitude of factors at play in any situation. Some fixed-mindset students actively sought out other students who did worse than themselves, in order to make themselves feel better. What they may be doing is essentially protecting the perception they have of themselves in their mind of being smart, clever and more intelligent than others. Worryingly in this regard was the fact that the fixed-mindset group said they would even consider cheating next time to improve their results.

The brain perhaps seeks to resolve this stress quickly by explaining away the results as bad luck, an unfair test perhaps, in order to cling to this fragile 'self-worth'. The stress referred to is termed cognitive dissonance.[55] It's the gap between what the facts tell us about a situation (e.g. our lack of performance at a particular activity) and the projected self-image we have about how good we are at it. Should the performance be perceived as bad and therefore at odds with our own perception, then stress is created (i.e. a dissonant outcome).

The stress is addressed, somewhat irrationally, by finding others who did equally bad or worse than you, and then forming a new social group to discuss how unfair the test was in order to elevate this stress. I've done this myself and it made me feel better in the short term, but it ignored or 'papered over the cracks' of the bigger problem; that is, I just wasn't working hard enough at the time.

---

55 *Cognitive dissonance*, Britannica dictionary. Available from www.britannica.com/science/cognitive-dissonance [accessed 2024].

I carried out a similar experiment myself at a conference recently in Belfast, Northern Ireland. Instead of maths tests, we distributed word anagrams to about 30 different business people attending the event. There were three words to unscramble and reassemble into new words. Of the three words, two were easy and one was more difficult.

Here's the twist: some of the participants got different words than the rest. These people had two impossible words and one difficult (but possible) word to solve. We spiced things up a little by giving these impossible words to high-achieving academic participants such as architects and accountants.

As the keynote speaker at the event, which was centred on motivation and improvement, I made sure to run the word tests at pace, to ensure participants had no time to compare notes. Every person at each round table got the same words. There were five tables. The table in the middle, surrounded by all the other tables, was the most interesting – this table received the two impossible words, together with one tough but possible word to solve.

I asked those who had solved the initial word to put their hands up. No hands were raised at the middle table. Then we instructed them to simply move on to the next word, as 'each word should only take a few seconds' (piling on the pressure).

As those at the surrounding tables raised their hands – solving an easy word such as 'melon' by converting it to 'lemon', those at the centre table struggled. They had easy-looking words such as 'while' to solve, but these of course were impossible anagrams. They glanced around as the hands went up. Again, the third word they had received was more difficult but solvable.

When questioned later, one of the participants at the centre table confessed that he didn't even attempt the third word. His confidence was shot at that point. Meanwhile, at the surrounding tables we had one or two who solved the third word. The question is: would they have solved it if they were seated at the centre table? Perhaps not.

Performance results shouldn't impact our self-worth. They're products of our attributes *multiplied* by focused effort over time. Do not underestimate the magnification power of focused hard work applied consistently over time. It's transformative and life-changing.

When we refer to tennis champions, we examine this mindset in a sport where there's no hiding place. It's you against your opponent and there's very little room to blame others.

In such contexts, what we tell ourselves now becomes of critical importance. Tennis coach Patrick Mouratoglou reflected on his success with some of the greatest athletes in the sport, such as Serena Williams. Together they won ten tennis grand slams. Mouratoglou prides himself on coaching a winning mindset. One surprising phenomenon he has encountered working with champions is that of 'tanking'.

Tanking

If our identity becomes entangled with our sport or profession, other negative consequences can also arise. Not only does a sensible strategic re-evaluation of our career path become inhibited (as we discussed in chapters regarding the tennis career of Mardy Fish), but so too can our performance.

Very talented athletes in tennis, for example, can begin to purposely miss shots and simply stop trying. Essentially, they're telling everyone that they're not interested in the match; they're not trying.

This sounds incredible given the sacrifices made by them and their support teams to get to that point. Nick Kyrgios, 2022 Wimbledon finalist, provides a great example. At the Shanghai Open in 2018 he was accused of tanking by the chair umpire before losing to world number 104 Bradley Klahn. At one point, Kyrgios simply walked off court as his opponent was about to return a shot to him. He walked to his seat without even glancing up at the return shot, to the boos of the crowd.

Coach Mouratoglou concludes, having had some first-hand experience of this with his players, that it's a protectionist mindset. If I don't try, then I'm not losing because the other player is better. Athletes, students, business people and those in all walks of life who have been told (and, as such, tell themselves) that they're talented, smart and exceptional seek to protect that self-image. Coach Mouratoglou overcame this issue with one of his athletes by being supportive, taking responsibility as a coach for the outcome and creating a bond with players that communicates that they're in this collectively, not on their own.

If we fail, we fail together. There's no shame in coming second, but we must always give everything we have on the court. Failure is not a reflection on us personally. Mastery is the pursuit of excellence in that discipline, whether we win, lose or draw.

This mindset also allows us to examine failure through a new lens. No longer is it the lens of 'I wasn't good enough', but the lens of mastery. With this changed mindset, it enables us to view failure as an opportunity for insight, a chance to identify areas for improvement in our performance and expedite our journey towards mastery. The highs and lows of emotion are just that. Ideally, we stand back and observe them rolling by like waves in the ocean, knowing that they will return to tranquil waters in the short term.

Finally, there should be no reflection on personal worth when we fail at one particular thing or another. Our lives are a mosaic of triumphs and failures.

Returning to the comparison we began with, Matti Nykänen and 'Eddie' Edwards, they had very different post-ski-jumping careers. Nykänen had a turbulent post-retirement from the sport. Marked by highs such as selling over 25,000 albums as a singer and lows such as time spent in prison for assault and severe financial troubles, he sadly died at the relatively young age of 55. Eddie the Eagle was welcomed back to Britain as a celebrity and, despite facing some financial troubles himself, went on to write a book, inspire a movie about his life and leverage his fame to engage in admirable charity work.

The lesson here is that our performance in one area does not define us as individuals. Mastery, in this sense, paints a broader picture that we should always keep in mind. With the right mindset we can begin to discern the wood from the trees and uncover a lifetime of opportunity and growth.

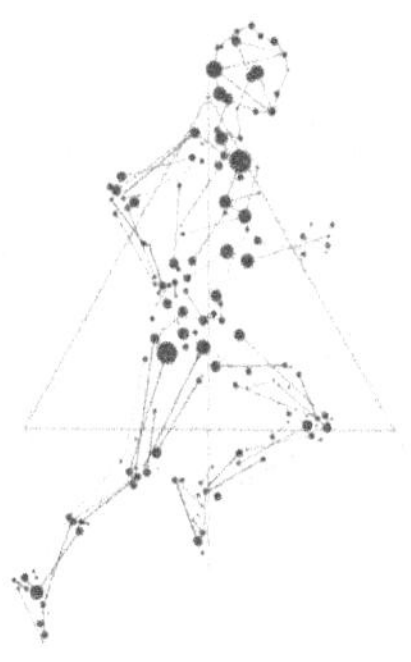

6 Increasing Your Luck

'Opportunity does not waste time with those who are unprepared.'

Idowu Koyenikan[56]

Belfast in 1983 was a city fragmenting under its own tumultuous history. Just to the south-west of the city centre lay the suburb of Dunmurry, primarily a residential area. A superstore called Crazy Prices stood as a semblance of normality in this local community. It offered a no-frills shopping experience, aligning with its budget-friendly ethos. It was a busy, local hub where people would do their weekly shopping and interact with each other. Today, glimpsing photographs of this bygone era feels like peering through a portal to an almost unrecognizable time. The bright oranges and browns of the shop's façade dominated the fashion trends of the 1980s. An era renowned for its embrace of eye-catching colours, symbolizing its unapologetic approach to style. It was a time when Belfast, scarred by the bloody conflict of the Troubles, saw its citizens navigate the mundane danger of everyday shopping.

This particular branch of Crazy Prices featured something special in its window: a shiny new bicycle. Not just any bicycle, but a Chopper, complete

[56] I. Koyenikan, *Wealth for All: Living a Life of Success at the Edge of Your Ability* (2016).

with a front basket, epitomizing the height of cool by the standards of the time.

Against this window stood a little girl, her eyes wide with wonder, drinking in the sight of the bicycle. It was a dream tethered just beyond reach. A prize in stark contrast to her family's financial reality, where even scraping together coins for the electricity meter was a daily struggle.

This bicycle, in all its unattainable glory, stood as a symbol of aspiration amid a backdrop of hardship. It was being raffled as part of a marketing promotion. The process to enter this draw was simple. First, make a purchase at the store – a trivial act in itself but money was in short supply. The second step, complete the phrase: 'Do your shopping at Crazy Prices because…' This was where the magic lay, an invitation to articulate why this ordinary place of commerce held some meaning for you.

Amid the throngs of shoppers each week, for this ten-year-old girl the odds of winning the bicycle of her dreams seemed astronomically stacked against her. Particularly given that she lived some two miles away and had to walk to the shop to make a purchase. In short, to win the bike she badly needed to increase her luck.

In this chapter we explore how luck played its part in the lives of some of the most successful people in history.

Preparing for luck

When the Battle of Austerlitz began in 1805 the French army was outnumbered. Napoleon Bonaparte had some 72,000 men and 157 cannons.[57] The enemy army had approximately 85,000 soldiers and 318 cannons.[58] It would become one of the most important military engagements of the Napoleonic Wars and the reshaping of Europe. Interestingly, the most decisive part of this battle would be… a stroke of luck. A foggy morning.

At around 8.45am on 2 December 1805, Napoleon observed a dense fog that had settled between his army and the target enemy position approximately one mile away. Their position would normally provide a clear view of Napoleon's

[57] A. Uffindell, *Great Generals of the Napoleonic Wars* (2003).

[58] Ibid. p. 19.

forces from a strategic height advantage, known as the Pratzen Heights, in modern-day Czechia. The Pratzen Heights had been abandoned by his army during an enemy advance just a few days earlier. The thick fog would now allow Napoleon to advance on the Pratzen Heights position undetected, winning a stunning victory that would ultimately split his opponents' army in two.

Yet, if we peer beyond the surface of the facts, a different narrative emerges. It's a story not solely of chance, but of astute awareness and strategic acumen. One where the fog becomes less of a lucky charm and more a testament to Napoleon's ability to harness an opportunity. Luck for Napoleon was not a mere whimsical benefactor. It was a complex interplay of preparation, anticipation and action.

The central component here was speed. Napoleon Bonaparte's ability to mobilize his troops quickly and effectively, to take advantage of the fog, can be attributed to several factors, including:

- His communication system, which was advanced for its time. He used a combination of messengers, signal flags and the semaphore telegraph system (a system of sending messages by holding the arms according to an alphabetic code). This allowed him to coordinate troop movements and respond to changing situations with remarkable speed.
- Napoleon's command structure was highly centralized, which meant decisions could be made quickly without the need for consultation with a large number of subordinates. This streamlined decision-making process enabled him to adapt to changing circumstances rapidly.
- The French army was also well-trained and disciplined. These troops were accustomed to rapid manoeuvres and could execute complex battle plans efficiently.

Napoleon was also present at the battle that morning to make key decisions – a morale boost in itself for his troops and a fact of which he was keenly aware. Unlike battles in the Second World War, for example, where decisions were being made over the telephone by Adolf Hitler several hundred miles away from the front, such as in the key Battle of Stalingrad. Napoleon was on top of real-time information. His plan was to recapture the Pratzen Heights and launch a decisive assault to the centre of the opposing army and encircle them from the rear. The French army thrust forward with around 16,000 troops, mostly on foot.

Crucially, how long the fog lasted would also be vital to Napoleon's plan. If his troops were uncovered too soon, the element of surprise would be gone, and if it lingered too long they would be unable to determine whether opposing troops had evacuated the Pratzen Heights, preventing him from executing his attack most efficiently. This final element is where true luck would play its part, but with meticulous preparation he had minimized most of the uncertainty. As it turned out, his retreat from the Pratzen Heights days earlier was all part of the plan.

The retreat was in fact a ruse to lure his enemies into thinking that his army was in a weakened state. As such, the bulk of enemy forces were strategically deployed elsewhere. Meanwhile, Napoleon's main army was to be concealed in a dead ground opposite the Pratzen Heights. The soldiers and commanders on top of the Heights were stunned to see so many French troops coming towards them, and after some intense fighting were forced to withdraw down the slopes. The plan had firmly turned the battle in France's favour.

Let's pause here to briefly unpack this as there are some important facts to note. Aspects of warfare always have an element of chance involved. The appearance of fog at just the right time was a fortunate circumstance for Napoleon, but he leveraged it to his full advantage. This included in-depth planning, particularly in terms of the terrain. This kind of fog, often seen in valleys and low-lying areas during colder months, can be predictable if one is familiar with the local geography and meteorological patterns. In fact, it's likely that he had studied the local climate and understood that the region where the Battle of Austerlitz took place was prone to morning fog, especially at that time of year (early December). Indeed, he's quoted as telling his officers prior to the Battle of Austerlitz, 'Gentlemen, examine this ground carefully, it is going to be a battlefield; you will have a part to play upon it.'[59]

---

[59] D. Chandler, *The Campaigns of Napoleon* (1966).

One final piece of preparation was also crucial, the selection of senior command. Napoleon was able to execute such a risky plan because one of his most capable and trusted military commanders, General Louis-Nicolas Davout, played a key decisive role at the flanks of the French advance. His leadership and tactical acumen were instrumental in the French victory. Napoleon had, in the years leading up to the battle, reformed the French military, emphasizing the promotion of officers based on merit rather than on nobility – a testament to his judgement of character and military skill.

Ultimately and perhaps most importantly, Napoleon's openness to learning and his outlook on life was the key factor. Years of preparation had enabled him to seize momentary advantages such as these. He was an avid reader of military history and theory. His studies of past military campaigns, particularly those of Alexander the Great, Julius Caesar and Frederick the Great, informed his understanding of warfare. Importantly, despite his many successes, Napoleon also faced setbacks and defeats. His ability to learn from these experiences, adjust his strategies and come back stronger was a key aspect of his military development. A military development that allowed Napoleon to conquer for a time an area larger than the entirety of the modern-day European Union.[60]

Distorted reality

In the Museum of Tolerance in Los Angeles there are two doors at the entrance. One is marked 'Prejudiced' and the second is marked 'not Prejudiced'. Those that attempt to open the latter door will find that it's locked. The entrance to the museum illustrates the point that we're *all* prejudiced in some way. We *all* experience bias as a result of our environment and upbringing. We're essentially conditioned in particular ways. This bias can be self-serving and it results in experiencing the world around us through many hundreds of potential conditioned lenses. These range from sunk cost fallacy (where we have a tendency to make poor decisions based on how much we've invested in a particular strategy already; for example, sometimes chasing losing investments), the Dunning-Kruger effect (cognitive bias in which

---

[60] *Napoleon summary,* Encyclopædia Britannica. Available from www.britannica.com/summary/Napoleon-I [accessed 23 December 2023].

people wrongly overestimate their knowledge or ability in a specific area), to numerous fears and phobias.[61] The result can be to misjudge information.[62]

An example of this is a story told by celebrated author Malcolm Gladwell. It's an example that's all the more important, given his great work and contributions to the study of psychological impediments to our success throughout his career. I'm a huge fan.

Gladwell was a journalist at the *Washington Post* in the early 1990s. He was approached many times during that period by a lobbyist and campaigner, Sid Wolfe, regarding what were the beginnings of the US opioid crisis, a surge of addiction to prescription drugs in the 1990s. Wolfe, who was a physician and the co-founder and director of Public Citizen's Health Research Group, campaigned for greater regulation of doctors in terms of prescribing addictive painkillers. Gladwell candidly admits that this is something he probably should have written about at the time in his influential column in the *Washington Post*, a newspaper that was and is so highly respected that it can have an impact on issues like this. Interestingly, Gladwell said of the omission, 'No one was more wrong than me on this issue, 100,000s of people have died in this country because we didn't pay attention to what you (Sid Wolfe) were saying in 1991.'[63]

This of course is an exaggeration; it wasn't Gladwell's fault. It's a point perhaps more appropriately directed at the disinterested mainstream media of the time. There's an important lesson here, however. He goes on to say that he and others considered Wolfe to be 'overbearing and hysterical', and his mistake was that he should have judged 'the message not the messenger'. 'I was blinded by my ideology, and it's a reminder of how dangerous having ideological convictions' can be.[64] His ideology was that of a conservative activist, perhaps considering at the time that drug companies were being

[61] J. Strough, L. Schlosnagle and L. DiDonato, 'Understanding decisions about sunk costs from older and younger adults' perspectives' in *The Journals of Gerontology: Series B 66B* 6, 681–686 (November 2011). Available from doi.org/10.1093/geronb/gbr057

[62] M. Mazor and S. Fleming, 'The Dunning-Kruger effect revisited' in *Nature Human Behaviour* 5, 677–678 (2021).

[63] M. Gladwell, *In Triplicate*. Revisionist History. Podcast. Season 7, Episode 3. Pushkin Industries.

[64] Ibid.

unfairly maligned. Something we've come to learn was not the case, unluckily for all involved, particularly the massive numbers of victims and addicts. In short, we all do better when we try to put prejudices aside and instead judge the message.

Lucky or unlucky

Dr Richard Wiseman, a professor of psychology at the University of Hertfordshire, England, has written several psychology books and is particularly known for his work on the nature of luck and its psychological aspects. He has extensively explored the concept of luck through various social experiments and has made significant contributions to the understanding of this elusive phenomenon. Contrary to the common belief that luck is a random and uncontrollable factor in people's lives, Wiseman's research suggests that individuals can significantly influence their own luck. His book, *The Luck Factor: Changing Your Luck, Changing Your Life, the Four Essential Principles*, presents the idea that luck is not merely a matter of chance but is greatly affected by people's attitudes and behaviours.[65] Through a series of experiments and workshops, he demonstrated that people often create their own luck through their mental attitudes and actions. For instance, in one experiment, Wiseman planted money on the ground and observed that (self-identifying) 'lucky' individuals were more likely to notice and pick up the money, whereas those who considered themselves unlucky often missed these opportunities.

Wiseman describes how our state of mind can affect our focus, and therefore impact what opportunities we're able to see. He describes it as being akin to a small, narrow spotlight that might show only a small proportion of your environment, while a soft-focus wider spotlight allows us to see a lot more at once. His research has found that if we're anxious about a situation or ourselves, our attentional spotlight becomes small, so we tend not to see the bigger picture. It's not a permanent state, of course, but rather a frame of mind, and can be changed.

---

[65] R. Wiseman, *The Luck Factor: Changing Your Luck, Changing Your Life, the Four Essential Principles* (2003).

This connection between mood and opportunity makes a lot of sense. Becoming overly focused on a particular outcome can simply shut out important random opportunities. Think of how this might work in your career. For example, perhaps I have my sights set on a job in a particular big law firm. If I, as a law graduate, focus too narrowly on this goal, it means I might miss excellent opportunities at other law firms, or with banks, insurance and tech companies. And what if the objective is to win a raffle for a bicycle in a shop window?

Increasing your luck

Our ten-year-old protagonist at the window was a little girl called Sharon. It's a true story. A story in which Sharon Magennis (who later became a very successful school principal in my local town of Clones, County Monaghan) and her younger sister Julie walked the two miles from her home to make small purchases in Crazy Prices, Dunmurry, to enter the draw each day. One day, however, she noticed something. Shoppers were being given the opportunity to enter the draw, but were not taking it. Discarded draw entry forms were left behind by busy and stressed-out parents, perhaps eager to leave the shop rather than spend the mental energy to complete the required marketing phrase: 'Do your shopping at Crazy Prices because…' It was an opportunity not wasted on Sharon. She filled out every entry form discarded by disinterested shoppers over a period of weeks, sometimes doing 20-odd forms per day. Entering a new finish to the required phrase each time, gradually swaying the odds more in her favour. The result? A winning entry form and the delivery of a brand-new bicycle, which just weeks earlier seemed totally out of reach.

Again, it's worth reflecting on the skills brought to bear on this situation. Chief among them, observing the discarded entry forms, the persistence to keep showing up each day and the creativity to come up with new phrases to enter in response to the question posed. Combined, they resulted in hundreds of entry forms submitted and a percentage representation in the draw vastly above Sharon's means. We can all learn much from this example of taking opportunities that others miss or lack the motivation to see through.

Summary

Our actions and behaviours can vastly affect the odds of achieving what we want, actions and behaviours such as the meticulous preparation and judgement of character displayed by Napoleon. Being conscious of our own biases and recognizing how invisible lenses can shape, and sometimes distort, outcomes for us and those around us. The ability to cast our observational spotlight wide and see the opportunities others miss. But more crucially, it's about possessing the courage – the bottle – to step through the door of opportunity when it presents itself and to fully leverage these skills. It's this blend of preparedness, perception and audacity that often sets apart the triumphant from the rest.

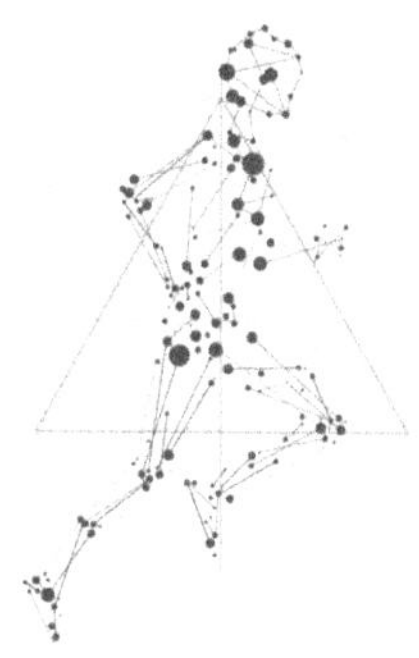

7

Never Lose Again

'It is impossible to live without failing at something, unless you live so cautiously that you might as well not have lived at all, in which case you fail by default.'

J.K. Rowling [66]

Mystery at Logan Airport

Step into the realm of Logan International Airport, Boston, and you're not just entering a transportation hub, you're stepping into a meticulously crafted theatre of security. Remember, this is the airport from which two of the hijacked planes of 11 September 2001 (9/11) took flight. That tragic day rewrote the script for airport security and transformed Logan into a fortress. Security at Logan, with its advanced technology and trained personnel, functions on a principle that transcends the physical. It operates on the idea that the best defence against chaos is not just rigorous checks, but the creation of a system so visibly thorough, so convincingly robust that it deters ill intentions before they can even manifest.

[66] J.K. Rowling, 'Harvard University commencement speech.' Harvard University, Cambridge, MA (June 2008).

It's a *psychological barrier* as much as a physical one. As travellers, we're part of this narrative. Our role is to comply and adapt. We remove our shoes, unpack our laptops and walk through body scanners, participating in a ritual that's as much about performance as it is about protection. In the early 2000s, travellers did just that. They got used to new procedures, binning liquids and water bottles, bagging other cosmetics. An odd thing began to occur, however.

Regardless of the increased compliance and adoption by passengers, it seemed that the level of checking and searching passenger bags didn't reduce as time went by. Increasing compliance and awareness of the dos and don'ts had little effect on the willingness of security staff to desist from finding potentially offensive objects.

This perhaps over-zealous searching didn't decrease, even though offensive objects, such as nail clippers and 100ml-plus containers of liquid began to become more elusive. The security staff, it seemed, were beginning to see shadows. Threats in the innocuous and mundane. And problems that didn't exist. It's all a product of lessons learned, a response to history's whispers.

Actually, it wasn't. Something more important and fundamental to human nature was driving this behaviour.

What's more, it's a problematic mindset that we all need to be aware of and at times take action to address. In part one of this book, we've looked at some key skills and insights to help us overcome challenges. In this chapter, we'll look at an important reason to *seek out* challenges. Reframing our imperfections and setbacks as tools for learning; driving us forwards towards a new horizon of personal development.

Risk and reward in evolution

In Josh Waitzkin's wonderful book, *The Art of Learning*, he delves deep into the process of learning. He considers the dilemma of the hermit crab.[67]

At its core, it's a story about risk and growth, encapsulated in the life of this unassuming sea creature. The hermit crab, ensconced in its shell, reaches a point where its domicile no longer fits. It's a moment of truth, where safety

---

[67] J. Waitzkin, *The Art of Learning: An Inner Journey to Optimal Performance* (2007).

and comfort clash with the need for expansion. The quest for a new shell is fraught with danger. The crab must abandon its familiar, snug shell and venture out, soft and unprotected, into a world teeming with threats.

This is the crab's gamble, an exposure of vulnerability in pursuit of something greater. It's a choice between the security of the known and the perilous allure of growth. And isn't that, in some strange way, a metaphor for our own lives? The moments when we must step out of our comfort zones, exposed and unguarded, to reach for a larger existence?

To take that analogy one step further, what about a sea creature with no protective shell at all?

Octopuses are often considered one of the most intelligent invertebrates. Their cognitive abilities show parallels with those seen in more traditionally recognized intelligent animals, such as some birds (e.g. crows, parrots) and mammals (e.g. dolphins, primates). This intelligence, which includes problem-solving abilities, use of tools and complex behaviours, is particularly intriguing given that they evolved separately from vertebrates that include humans and primates.

There are several theories as to why, including the fact that they inhabit diverse and challenging environments, from coral reefs to the open ocean. One of the key factors, however, is that they lack physical defences. Unlike many other marine animals, they don't have a hard shell or spiny exoskeleton for protection. Their soft bodies make them vulnerable to predators. As a result, evolution favoured the development of intelligence as a means of survival, allowing octopuses to use cunning and adaptability to avoid predators and use tools for defence.

In the Oscar-winning documentary, *My Octopus Teacher*, we're shown the amazing ways an octopus uses its intelligence, such as camouflaging itself, surrounding itself with seashells, and at one point distracting a shark that's viciously attacking it, to place itself on the shark's back, the safest place.[68]

By living on their wits, so to speak, as opposed to having physical defences, they're constantly under challenge. As a result, 150 to 200 million years of

[68] P. Ehrlich and J. Reed, dirs., *My Octopus Teacher* (2020).

evolution has facilitated the development of remarkable skills. If we want a metaphor for the benefit of pushing ourselves, this is it.[69]

The octopus lives pretty much its entire life outside its comfort zone and has become possibly the most remarkable creature on the planet.

Seeking challenge

The RTE (Raidió Teilifís Éireann) cameras were ready to roll. RTE is the national TV broadcaster in Ireland. I was standing in a room at the Peace Link sports complex in my home town of Clones, County Monaghan, with, as it happens, a former teacher of mine, Jim O'Connor (the chairman of the Peace Link Sports Facility at the time).

Jim is an absolute gentleman and one of the best teachers I ever had. RTE was filming what would be a prime-time programme that would be shown numerous times over the following years, with audience figures over 200,000. Jim and I were about to do separate interviews for the show, all in our native Irish language.

The embarrassing problem I had was that, despite years of schooling in the subject and professional exams taken and passed in my early 20s, I really didn't understand more than a few phrases of Irish. I had no concept of future, present or past tense and the nuances of the language to enable me to complete the interview competently. The funny thing was, I think Jim could have been more nervous than I was. Probably because I had one thing that was going to help me through this, which I'll explain below.

Months earlier I had been contacted, in my capacity as public relations officer for Baseball Ireland, by an RTE producer. I know what you're thinking: yes, there is a baseball league in Ireland. But, back to the scenario at hand. From what I understood, the TV crew had to record 50% of the programme in Irish, because the show (*An Geansaí*) was designed to support and showcase minority sports and promote the Irish language.

We had struggled to canvas volunteers for interviews, so I put my hand up for one, on the basis that they would bring the cameras to my hometown baseball

---

69 N. Landman *et al.*, *Cephalopods Present and Past: New Insights and Fresh Perspectives* (2007).

club in Clones. The reason I thought I could get through an interview was that I had been practising and teaching a memory association technique for many year – mostly to law students. My plan was to get a list of the questions from RTE that they wanted answers to, in Irish, and write out my answers in English. I then proceeded to have these translated into Irish.

I then went on to learn these Irish translations phonetically, in order to be prepared to repeat the answer (like a parrot) for the interview. These memory association techniques had considerably helped my exam success as a law student and they had become second nature to me after some 20 years of practice. I had, however, been partially scuppered earlier on the day of the interview when we visited a school locally with the RTE film crew. The producer asked if I could take some of the questions out of context at the school. I had to decline (not sharing the reason why) as I hadn't fully finished memorizing them.

When the interview eventually began, the producer kept asking me to look at the camera when I was answering the questions, but I couldn't. Despite firing out all the answers in Irish, I needed to access the visual memory part of my brain, which meant (if you watch someone trying to visually remember anything) I was looking up to the left side – which I find is essential for visualization.

It was tough but I got through the interview and thankfully they seemed happy. I was then delighted to be asked to repeat it all in English, which I did. Again thankfully, the English version was all they aired on the show months later and it was a big hit. They did air Jim's interview in Irish which was, of course, in great shape compared to my version of Irish phonetic garble.

Why is this relevant?

I think it's so important to push ourselves, mind and body, to develop new skills. The hermit crab and octopus analogies are relevant here. It was easy to fail at this. I knew that it was a success just getting the cameras to Clones to promote the club, regardless of whether my interview would ever make the cut.

I had no problem being embarrassed by my shortcomings in Irish because I had an overarching purpose. The experience bolstered my confidence in doing other national shows on radio, etc. because they were in English and I also had this tough experience to fall back on as a reference point.

I would say to myself prior to any interview, 'Nothing could be that hard again.' I suppose this is a form of 'referential confidence'; that is, 'trust' in myself (which is the etymology for this word). Based on past experience. This is just a small example of how growth and confidence can occur by pushing ourselves into uncomfortable situations – looking for that new shell or abandoning it altogether.

Mindset and challenge

As we push ourselves to improve it's easy to fall into a trap. A mindset trap that focuses not on expanding our comfort zone or the horizon of growth, where the true win lies, but instead on our fragile self-worth, mixed up in the outcome of one miniature task or another.

Let's return for a moment to an example we looked at in Chapter 5 – Mastery. In that chapter we discussed an experiment conducted in a hotel in Belfast involving attendees at a business seminar. You may recall that the objective of the exercise was to demonstrate to those present the debilitating and demotivating power of cognitive dissonance. You may also recall that one table in the middle had two impossible words to solve as anagrams, while the surrounding tables had easier words to solve. All tables had a third word that was difficult but solvable. The distraction of not being able to solve the first two words, coupled with the fact that others seated at the surrounding tables could, evidenced by them raising their hands, created anxiety.

This created a demand on cognitive resources. We perhaps begin to think more about why we can't solve these words. Words that others can solve easily. We become self-conscious about our perceived model of ourselves as good at a particular thing that's now at odds with facts the world is presenting to us. This internal conflict is very distracting and clouds our otherwise clear-thinking brain.

You might be tempted to brush off this example as an unfounded theory. However, when you're in these circumstances you know just how dreadful that feeling is. Falling behind, knowing others are performing better.

The point is to allow us to experience the concept and recognize it as an issue to be aware of. Like many emotions, if we can label it and be aware of the circumstances that can create it, it becomes easier to manage. The point is, when we allow our mind to become tangled in the emotion of one short-term outcome, we lose sight of the larger problem. The larger problem is the consequences of failing to push ourselves towards the horizon of growth.

Logan Airport and prevalence-induced concept change in human judgement

The behaviour of airport security in the early 2000s prompted research. Professor Daniel Levari and his colleagues at Harvard University looked more closely and discovered a concept called 'prevalence-induced concept change in human judgement'.[70]

It's essentially a function of brain efficiency. Our brain uses comparisons with previous information instead of re-evaluating things from the start. The latter needs much more brain power. As such, the reason they concluded that airport security continued searching passenger bags at the same level, even though compliance had risen significantly, was that they were now looking for problems where none existed. Or to put it another way, they were suffering from 'problem creep'. The research suggests that the 'brain computes the value of most stimuli by comparing them to other relevant stimuli'.[71]

It therefore demonstrates that when we fail to challenge ourselves to improve and find new skills, there can be a tendency to regress. This regression can include today's comforts becoming tomorrow's discomforts, which are spelled out in many convincing examples in Michael Easter's book, *The Comfort Crisis*.[72]

---

[70] D. Levari *et al.*, 'Prevalence-induced concept change in human judgment' in *Science*, 360 (6396), 1465–1467 (2018).

[71] For further reading on this, see T. Hare *et al.*, 'Transformation of stimulus value signals into motor commands during simple choice' in *Proceedings of the National Academy of Sciences* 108 (44), 18120–18125 (2011).

[72] M. Easter, *The Comfort Crisis: Embrace Discomfort to Reclaim Your Wild, Happy, Healthy Self* (2021).

We've all experienced this to some extent. We worry about problems that aren't real and might never happen. Over time, as our comfort zone shrinks, we can procrastinate about problems as simple as making a phone call.

Police in various jurisdictions have experienced this in terms of neighbourhood watch initiatives. Reports gradually become more mundane as instances of crime reduce. To recognize the risks of how our brain efficiency mechanism can inhibit us living our lives is a scary thought. To combat this we should perhaps seek out positive, measured and productive challenges that further our experience of life and boost our knowledge and skills.

In short, the only way to actually fail ourselves is to stop pushing ourselves towards improvement and the full experience life has to offer. Do that and you'll never really lose again.

Summary

In short, there's a lot we can learn from our octopus teachers.

Part 2
Balance

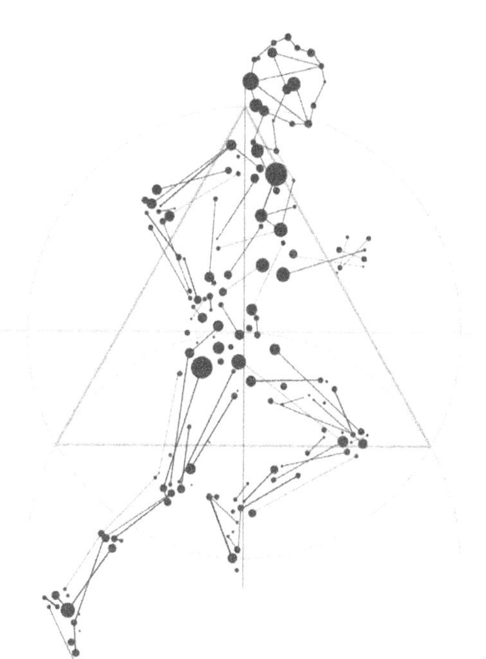

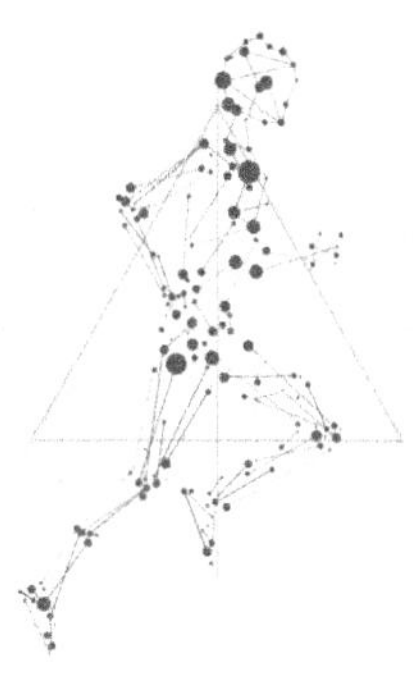

8
Opportunity: Balanced with Integrity

'Man cannot discover new oceans unless he has the courage to lose sight of the shore.'

André Gide[73]

Holidaymakers generally avoid visiting Singapore in November; temperatures can exceed 30°C and there's often heavy rain. However, on 20 November 1995, Singapore airport was perhaps as busy as it has ever been. Hordes of media and onlookers thronged the arrivals hall, barely restrained by the flimsy cordons. First to exit from the arrival doors, which resembled a plush hotel lobby, were six to eight blue-uniformed police officers with sidearms. Following them, a TV camera hoisted on the shoulder of a news crew member, hurrying to ensure that not a moment of this unique scene was missed. Maybe 20 formally suited officious-looking men followed, some on phones and others gesturing directions towards more police officers.

And at the centre of this melée, hunched over and walking briskly, was a 20-something Englishman wearing a black baseball cap turned backwards, a green jumper and sweatpants. He wore white trainers and white socks pulled

[73] French author and winner of the Nobel Prize in Literature in 1947.

halfway up his lower legs on the outside of his sweatpants, resembling a skinny pale executive attempting to dress appropriately for his first gym visit in many years.

The flashes and clicks of the cameras and the shouts of the reporters echoed in an otherwise eerily quiet scene. As the group neared the end of the gauntlet of media heckling, the young man looked up with a cheeky smirk; it was the totally miscued reaction of someone unable to comprehend a level of media attention normally reserved for global superstars. Nick Leeson, former high-powered banker, had returned to the exotic new frontier of financial markets – Singapore. This time to face trial for an £830 million fraud that had bankrupted one of the UK's oldest merchant banks.

Regarding André Gide's quote above, it's true that sometimes we must push ourselves into the unknown in order to discover new opportunities or indeed new things about ourselves. Leeson's story adds a significant word of caution, however. Losing sight of the shore does not mean losing sight of our values and integrity. The latter should be stowed for our journey, ready and able to guide us through troubled waters.

A lapse of integrity can mean so many things. I worked as a criminal solicitor for over six years in a criminal law practice close to the border between Northern Ireland and the Republic of Ireland. The criminals we represented had done it all, from traffic violations to the most extreme offences such as murder and rape. The reasons varied but, commonly, the more severe offenders had drink and drug problems, abusive upbringings, poor education levels, financial difficulties and typically a close social connection with many who had the same problems.

The misguided motivations of white-collar criminals can be much more puzzling. Far from living harsh lives, these are criminals who generally live a comfortable and privileged existence. In most cases, these are individuals without prior instances of fraud, who find themselves in a position of opportunity and ultimately stray from the path of integrity. Generally, the need to steal to support basic lifestyle needs is absent. Rather, what we tend to see is the commission of an unnecessary crime; for example, a theft of money within a business context, where the individual was in fact throwing away an abundance of legitimate opportunity in favour of short-term gain.

Of all fraud cases committed, white-collar crime tends to be in the low minority. The extent of financial damage can be mind-boggling, as we'll see in the next chapter, when we examine the impact of fraudulent cultures, for example, in the 2008 global financial crash.

In this chapter, we'll attempt to understand more about why individuals perpetrate white-collar crime. This is important to understand in order to address the dangers posed for those who may fail to sustain their success in the long term, by straying from key personal values.

Opportunity

There have been many studies carried out on the subject of fraud, both at an organizational level, termed corporate crime, and at an individual level within an organization, termed occupational crime. One research study carried out sought to establish key characteristics of white-collar criminals, using a sample of 1,142 occupational fraud cases.[74] These characteristics usually include a high degree of education, specific knowledge obtained in the context of their duties within the organization, resulting in a level of rank that bestows trust and that other key ingredient, opportunity. This can lead to less oversight of the individual, who has built up trust with clients, employers, financiers, etc.

Many studies have also been carried out on the motives of offenders. Given an opportunity, typically the offender must have an incentive or be suffering from compulsion or pressure, and they must be able to rationalize their criminal behaviour to themselves. Opportunity, compulsion and rationalization are known as the fraud triangle.[75] Internal and external factors are of course at play when it comes to motivation. External factors can be pressure from others, particularly where a culture of wrongdoing surrounds an individual. Internal factors can include emotional deprivation, caused by a perceived lack of recognition, appreciation, demotion, rejection, etc., all of which can lead to frustration and ultimately the fraudulent act itself.

---

[74] See K. Holtfreter, 'Is occupational fraud "typical" white-collar crime? A comparison of individual and organisational characteristics' in *Journal of Criminal Justice* 33 (2005).

[75] D. Cressey, *Criminal Organization: Its Elementary Forms* (1972).

In the context of success, another internal motivation is very relevant: that of exaggerated aspirations. For example, for persons overly interested in money and a material value system, research has shown a heightened risk of white-collar crime.

Nick Leeson and Barings Bank: a case study in financial crime

Skill and opportunity are particularly relevant in the story of one of the most famous fraud cases in history, that of Nick Leeson. Leeson was responsible for an £830 million fraud that led to the downfall of Barings Bank.

Leeson was from a working-class background and grew up on a council estate in Watford, Hertfordshire, England. His father was a plasterer and his mother was a nurse. The bank he would ultimately defraud was founded in 1762 and had been run by the same family for over two centuries. The Baring family was related to the highest echelons of society, including Princess Diana. The power of Barings Bank lay in its name. It could raise capital on the best of terms because everyone knew that its clients were the cream of British society. Even the Queen held a bank account with Barings. It had a reputation as a discreet, safe bank with a deep sense of superiority over its competitor banks in the market.

Leeson finished sixth form in 1985 with six O Levels and two A Level passes, in English literature and history, with C and D grades, interestingly failing his third subject, mathematics.[76] He began his career in banking as a clerk with Coutts private bank, carrying out basic administration work such as crediting and debiting client accounts.

Leeson moved to Morgan Stanley's Futures and Options back office, clearing and settling listed derivatives transactions, and he later joined Barings Bank in 1989. He was briefly sent to help with problems in the Barings back office in Jakarta, where he carried out impressive work. He returned to London in September 1991 to investigate a case of fraud in which a Barings employee had used a client's account to trade on a proprietary basis until margin calls from the clearing houses unravelled the scheme. The task of fraud

[76] J. Rawnsley, *Total Risk: Nick Leeson and the Fall of Barings Bank* (1996).

investigator, even in a support role, allowed him to gain specialist knowledge and insight in the bank's inner workings; skills that would later help him sustain his vast fraud.

In 1986, UK Prime Minister Margaret Thatcher had deregulated the City of London, and the old division between banks and stockbrokers was removed. Stockbrokers replaced the image of gentlemanly bankers. It's probably not an overstatement to say that in the next few years this created a new open and accepted environment of brash, feverish money-making and greed. Greed was cool and material gain was the accepted measure of success, particularly in the City of London. In this environment, Barings Bank, the secure bank at the heart of the British establishment, sought to cash in on the changing times.

Leeson initially worked for Barings' securities department. In 1986 this department had comprised a small team of stockbrokers, but by 1991 they contributed over half of the bank's profits. Leeson, years later, said that he had never heard of the bank before he went to work for it – there was no Barings in Watford. A point that illustrates perhaps different worlds meeting for the first time in this new trading environment.

Barings decided to open a futures and options office in Singapore in 1992. Leeson was appointed general manager, a huge opportunity and reward for his hard work in Jakarta and on other assignments. In this role Leeson would manage both the front and back office of Barings' trading operation in Singapore. In doing this, Barings circumvented normal accounting, internal control and audit safeguards. These positions would normally have been held by two different employees. This approach somewhat evidences the new cavalier attitude of banks, which sought to stop too much regulation getting in the way of making money. With little or no supervision from London, this arrangement would later make it easier for Leeson to hide critical information from his employers.

On the hectic trading floor in Singapore, mistakes were made by his new team. Like selling instead of buying stock, as instructed by clients. Mistakes in this context were easily made, with an incorrect hand signal, for example, to other traders on the floor. Leeson had a choice: tell head office, which is what he was supposed to do, or try to hide the losses.

He chose to hide the losses.

In the beginning his motive appeared to be out of fear. Fear of the operation in Singapore being closed and his being demoted back to a boring clerk's job within Barings. Leeson, using his specialist knowledge of how the bank worked, hid the losses in what would become the famous 88888 account.

The amounts started relatively small, thousands of dollars, but huge market movements exaggerated the losses, with the Nikkei rising as much as 1,000 points per day around that time.[77]

The gap between what the client was supposed to have bought and the fact they had sold instead widened dramatically. The mess was compounded by practically no oversight, which enabled Leeson to manipulate the bank's software to hide the losses. These losses quickly increased to millions of pounds. Remarkably, Leeson exacerbated the situation by reporting losses as profits to head office.

One other key oversight failure related to margin payments. To make trades, Leeson's team had to make margin payments for trades, which in theory would later be recouped from the bank's clients. The problem was that the clients didn't exist, as Leeson was using the bank's own money. The basic oversight mistake by the bank was that they didn't check that the money was coming back to them via client payments. This would have been easy to check, and Leeson himself later reported that he expected his scheme to all fall apart within days. This did not happen. As such, Leeson went on hiding his mistakes and attempting to trade out of this situation.

He was in too deep to come clean and instead doubled down by buying hundreds of unauthorized trades. By 1993 the market turned in his favour and he cleared losses in the region of £6 million. He was out of trouble.

Then something remarkable happened. The very next week he started to do it again. This time it was different. He didn't need to hide any mistake by him or a team member. Instead, the 88888 account was used not to hide losses but rather to deliberately perpetrate a fraud, which included selling cut-price stocks to clients.

Losses mounted into multiples of what Leeson had previously covered up. He survived key internal audits of his office, where he regarded the missed

---

[77] The Nikkei 225, or the Nikkei Stock Average, more commonly called the Nikkei or the Nikkei index – a stock market index for the Tokyo Stock Exchange.

discovery of approximately £100 million in losses as amazing. On how this escaped the notice of the auditors, Leeson later stated that 'a lot of them are just bumbling fools', regarding the hierarchy at Barings Bank. The result: a bankrupt bank, huge losses and prison for Leeson.

Understanding white-collar crime

There's a lot we can glean from the story of Leeson and Barings Bank. Here are a few key observations:

- The circumstances (particularly the lack of accountability) presented Leeson with the opportunity.
- Leeson had the skills and knowledge he needed and, perhaps more importantly, had the kind of personality or personal values that allowed him to conceive and carry out these schemes.
- The initial pressure of needing to 'succeed' provided the motivation for Leeson to take the risk.

That all makes sense, but let's look a little deeper into the personal motivation of Leeson.

Personality

Peter Norris, CEO of Barings Bank at the time the fraud was perpetrated, described Leeson as 'a highly intelligent creature, with a highly developed skill in manipulating the people around him'.[78] We know from our examination of the subject earlier in this book that IQ helps but only gets you so far. Leeson demonstrated other skills (which we referred to as PGQ in Chapter 2) such as charm, guile, persistence, influence. The sort of skills that can help anyone reach their goals in life. He also had the work ethic that makes all the difference in terms of the application of those skills. Sadly, he applied them in the wrong way. Leeson either did not value integrity and long-term sustainable success in the first place, or he buckled under the pressure and chose to compromise those values.

---

[78] *Inside Story Special: £830,000,000 – Nick Leeson and the Fall of the House of Barings*, YouTube video, at 22.30 mins. Posted by 'Wolfe' (23 January 2018). Available from www.youtube.com/watch?v=CkhcpcuZvV4

Motivation

So, fraud needs the right circumstances to happen, and it needs the right personality traits or personal value judgements in the person with the opportunity. Even so, taking a risk like this usually needs a strong motivation to trigger that compromise of integrity – and here we come to perhaps the most fascinating part of understanding white-collar crime. What is it that motivates people to commit fraud?

To understand this further, let's look at a German study that involved interviewing 60 convicted corporate criminals and 11 German public prosecutors.[79] From the information it gathered, the study outlined some typical phases of a white-collar crime:

- In phase one they try legally to achieve their private and professional goals.
- In phase two they realize that they haven't attained the success they hoped for, which paves the way for shame and fear.
- Phase three involves sounding out other ways of achieving success, which includes those on the margins of legality.
- Phase four is the initial act of fraud. If this is materially successful, it confirms and reinforces the perpetrator's justification of their actions to themselves.
- Phase five is the point of no return, in which the offender's personal sense of right and wrong is adapted to fit their circumstances, which further enables them to rationalize their actions. Those affected begin to lose touch with reality and become more deeply entangled in their actions.
- The sixth and final phase involves the discovery of the deed and the shock of reality – the offender faces the consequences of their actions, and (often) loses the rationalization of their actions.

We can see here that it's phase four that's the really key one in this process. It's here that the opportunity and personality combine and the compulsion

---

[79] T. Cleff *et al.*, 'Motives behind white-collar crime: results of a quantitative and qualitative study in Germany' in *Society and Business Review* (2013).

increases to the point where the choice is made to cross the line. The first choice then justifies all the later ones: Leeson's actions in covering up the initial mistakes of his team and recovering from a £6 million loss must certainly have had the effect of confirming and reinforcing his approach to running the high-risk 88888 account. Importantly though, the study notes that the process described does not always result in a crime. People experiencing the phases may instead choose to resist the fraudulent act itself; the study describes this as being due to 'internal factors such as the individual's personality structure and values'. Clearly, this is a choice that people make.

And that choice is not always about money: the 2013 German study concluded that '[t]he pursuit of money is only an ostensible need here, which is instrumental to satisfying the real, more deep-lying needs' of the individual. For Leeson, money was a factor but, perhaps more importantly, he also became a rock star in the financial world. He was manifesting an outcome that came from a deep-seated need to prove something.[b] He was showered with praise and awards. He was living the life of his dreams... until it all came tumbling down. That's what he gained and that's what he lost. While awaiting trial for the offences, Leeson was asked why this had all happened. He responded, 'It was a combination of errors. I should have referred it to people and I didn't.'[80]

There's a powerful clue in that answer: perhaps if he had asked for help when it all first started to go wrong, the chain of events would never have been triggered. He could have avoided that crucial phase four by reaching out and asking for help. The latter is of course made more difficult where individuals are entwined in a culture of fraud, as we'll see a little later in this book.

Conclusion

Oversight gaps can create a burden on employee morality that not everyone can respond well to, in terms of acting with virtue. Money tends, typically, not to be the primary motivator in individuals who can seek to fulfil some deep-seated perceived inadequacy through fraudulent activity.

---

[80] *Inside Story Special: £830,000,000 – Nick Leeson and the Fall of the House of Barings*, YouTube video, at 22.30 mins. Posted by 'Wolfe' (23 January 2018). Available from www.youtube.com/watch?v=CkhcpcuZvV4

Fraudulent acts tend to start with minor breaches of an individual's internal value structure, becoming normalized and rationalized over time.[81] The greater the distance from the victim in emotional terms, the easier acts of fraud can be perpetrated. As such, on recognizing these circumstances, our value system should be on high alert. Finally, an important takeaway is that the ability to resist the phases of fraudulent mindset is particularly enhanced with the ability to seek help and test our judgement with reference to role models and advisors that we can trust. The question then arises: what if we're part of a large corrupt organization? Something we delve into in our next chapter.

[81] E. Soltes, *Why They Do It: Inside the Mind of the White-Collar Criminal* (2019).

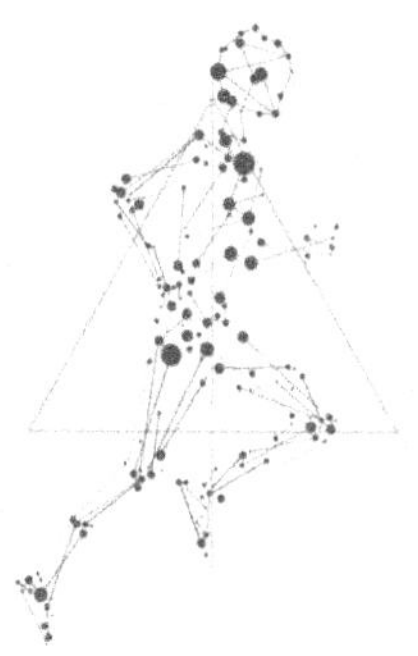

9

Collective Opportunity: Balanced with Integrity

'Winning isn't everything, it's the only thing.'[82]

Green Bay Packers Coach, Vince Lombardi

Hang-ups and impediments to our personal success journey can be many and varied. As we've seen in the previous chapter, a high degree of education, motivation and talent are by no means a guarantee of a successful career outcome. We now turn our attention to how we behave in groups or organizations. Furthermore, we also look at the influence that culture exercises over our personal value systems. Indeed, we may start our careers with a strong 'due north' on our metaphorical moral compass, but we commonly underestimate how the gravitational pull of group norms can distort our sense of direction.

A persuasive example of this is the case of front-line health care workers. We consider these some of the most highly educated and trustworthy people in society. Even more so for doctors working in the local community. However, in the United States during the late 1990s, if you attended your local doctor complaining of pain, you would have probably been prescribed something

[82] D. Maraniss, *When Pride Still Mattered: A Life of Vince Lombardi* (2000).

that stood a good chance of causing your death. Opioids at that time were being prescribed for the most modest of pain ailments and they carried a huge risk of addiction, death and destruction of the family and business lives of their victims.

Purdue Pharma played a significant role in the opioid crisis. The company is widely recognized for its aggressive marketing of Oxycontin, a powerful opioid painkiller, which was introduced in 1996. It was a catastrophe that saw needless deaths from opioid addiction, passing the 800,000-person mark in the US alone, from 1996 to present day. At the heart of this astonishing death toll was a mystery.

During the same period, certain US states would average around 36% fewer drug overdose deaths and 44% fewer opioid deaths than other US states. These were California, Idaho, Illinois, New York and Texas. Were these states more morally upstanding or perhaps resistant to the marketing ploys of the opioid painkillers in the marketplace? No. The answer instead is something much more interesting and comes down to the power of culture and human nature.

In this chapter, we'll look at the remarkable effect culture has on individuals. This extends further than to those directly engaged within an organization. Its reach, in fact, expands also to those within its cultural orbit.

Lost… along the way

Imagine you're in a game of 'corporate culture detective'. Each clue, seemingly trivial, offers a deeper insight into the organization's soul. It's found perhaps initially in the tone and practised nature of the office reception staff. Or a simple shrug, a fleeting look of disapproval at a decision to be made. Threads, when woven together over time, create a tapestry of workplace norms and values. Subtleties, repeated and witnessed, gradually stitch together the standard of what's acceptable and what's not. Nuances that ripple in a pond, expanding to shape behaviours and attitudes. Slowly, almost imperceptibly, these patterns condition an organization and the individuals within it to embrace important foundational values.

Back in 1992 I worked in a turkey factory during the summer while I was still at school. I remember working in the packing area of the factory. The manager needed turkeys of a particular weight for supermarket orders. I'll never forget weighing a particular packaged turkey. The manager said, 'Hold it there.' He leaned over me and pressed the print option about five times in order to produce labels for other packaged turkeys that were not the correct weight. It was a small thing perhaps, but it was a sign of what was acceptable in that culture.

Perhaps it was just an efficient way of getting things done, I rationalized to myself. Let's pause here, because the last four words of the previous sentence are probably the most important… *I rationalized to myself.*

Integrity

One of the most successful investors of all time, Warren Buffett, once said, 'In looking for people to hire, look for three qualities: integrity, intelligence, and energy. And if they don't have the first, the other two will kill you.'[83]

The selection of individuals is critically important, but something all too often overlooked is the effect of the culture we expose these individuals to. The fact is, when cultural norms are askew, it's like a tidal force acting on an object, it erodes values and has a remarkable effect on behaviour.

Clues to cultural group norms are sometimes subtle. But it doesn't take a corporate culture detective to see a change in culture if there's a huge banner hanging in the entrance to an office that says: FROM THE WORLD'S LEADING ENERGY COMPANY – TO THE WORLD'S LEADING COMPANY. The office belonged to Enron and, in fact, this wasn't *just* a change of culture, it was a declaration of war.

Enron Corporation is one of the most damning examples of cultural change. A change that ultimately resulted in its implosion in 2001. The Enron bankruptcy was the largest in US history at that time. The scale of financial loss was massive, impacting shareholders, employees and creditors. Thousands of employees lost their jobs and many more saw their retirement savings, largely composed of Enron stock, wiped out.

The loss to employees wasn't just financial but also reputational, as many found it difficult to find employment afterwards due to their association with

[83] W. Buffett, *In looking for people to hire, look for three qualities…* A–Z Quotes. Available from www.azquotes.com/quote/522299 [accessed December 2023].

Enron. Shareholders lost nearly $11 billion as Enron's stock price plummeted from over $90 per share in the mid-2000s to less than $1 by the end of November 2001.

Enron's collapse sent shockwaves through the energy markets and the broader financial world. It undermined investor confidence in corporate governance and accounting practices in the United States. To understand what happened at Enron let's start by looking at an individual.

In the world of high school academia, Jeff Skilling was something of an anomaly – a student whose brilliance in the classroom was matched only by his penchant for risk-taking, a trait that would later come to define his tenure at the helm of Enron.

At Harvard Business School, a place where the cream of the intellectual crop competes for supremacy, Skilling didn't just participate, he dominated. His performance there led him straight to the doors of McKinsey & Company in Houston.

It was here, amid the world of high-stakes corporate consulting, that Skilling's unique blend of intellect and boldness caught the eye of Ken Lay. Skilling's big idea – a 'Gas Bank' – was nothing short of revolutionary, capitalizing on the perennial mismatch between short-term supply and demand in the gas industry.

The success of this idea was so immediate and so compelling that Lay couldn't help but bring Skilling on board at Enron, first as the head of its trading operations at Enron Finance Corporation and later, in a move that would change the course of the company, as its CEO.

Under Skilling's leadership, Enron underwent a transformation as dramatic as it was rapid, shifting from a traditional energy company to a behemoth of financial trading. Enron's focus turned to trading energy futures and an array of other financial commodities, from broadband to fibre optics and even to paper goods.

By the year 2000, Enron was almost unrecognizable from its 1996 self. Trading operations now generated a staggering 99% of its income. Revenue had ballooned from $11,904 million to an astronomical $100,000 million.

Skilling's approach was simple: win at any cost. It began with the selection of staff. Skilling was on the hunt for a very specific type of employee – one that was not just smart, but also aggressive, with a capacity for ruthlessness in trading. The recruitment process at Enron under Skilling was akin to a filter, sifting through the country's talent pool to find those who fit his stringent criteria. Only the 'best and the brightest' were considered – traders, bankers, tech wizards, programmers, financial engineers – predominantly alumni of the Ivy Leagues and other prestigious institutions. It was a recruitment drive on steroids, pulling in between 250 and 500 fresh Master of Business Administration graduates every year.

Promotions and transfers within Enron were fast-paced, a whirlwind. The process left little room for learning the ropes or understanding the finer details of the industry. This relentless pace, combined with a cutthroat culture where those who couldn't keep up were quickly shown the door, set the stage for an environment where success was paramount, and the means to achieve it were secondary.

Skilling reshaped Enron's culture to not just accept but celebrate the art of skirting the edge of legality and ethics. Skilling's Enron emphasized 'creative risk-taking' and 'revolution' in the workplace. It wasn't just about pushing boundaries, it was about redrawing them entirely, often at the cost of legal and ethical integrity.

His leadership style created a dangerous pressure point within the organization – a resistance to bad news. In this world, the flow of information was not just controlled but contorted, both internally and externally. The disincentive to share unfavourable news or dissenting opinions led to an echo chamber where only success was acknowledged, and failure was either hidden away or repackaged as a triumph.

Frogs in hot water

To 'boil a frog in water' is a sort of parable phrase associated with the danger of gradual change. The idea is that if a frog is put in boiling water it will immediately jump out. However, if it's placed in cool water that's slowly heated it won't perceive the danger and will sadly be cooked to death. This metaphor is often used to illustrate how people can become complacent or unaware of slowly developing threats or problems. Let's look at this in the context of Enron, putting ourselves in the position of an employee there for a moment.

Sherron Watkins had worked extremely hard and secured a job at the prestigious Enron (later awarded 'America's Most Innovative Company' six years in a row by *Fortune* magazine).[84] She had carved a career path as a Certified Public Accountant, beginning in 1982 at Arthur Andersen, splitting her formative years between the hum of Houston and the buzz of New York. Starting in 1993, her role at Enron was not just one of involvement but of immersion. As Vice-President of Corporate Development she found herself at the very heart of the corporation, an unwitting witness to a saga that would unfold in the most dramatic of fashions.

It was at the dawn of 2002 when Watkins found herself in the glaring spotlight of national attention, summoned to testify before the august assemblies of the US House of Representatives and Senate. Her testimony was not just a recollection of events but a revelation of her forewarnings to Enron's CEO Kenneth Lay about the labyrinthine accounting irregularities that veiled the true state of the corporation's financial health.

Watkins' story underscores the delicate interplay of ambition, morality and the often unseen consequences of unchecked corporate machinations.

That's an important detail. Watkins was a whistleblower, which tells us she had a strong moral compass, which ultimately did shine through. It might not have been that way, though, as she would admit herself. She may never have had that opportunity, and probably on reflection should have left the corporation in the mid to late 1990s when it became clear how hot the water was getting. But she didn't, so why not?

In her book, *Power Failure: The Inside Story of the Collapse of Enron*, she talks in detail about the culture and the hold that culture had over their vast pool of employees.[85]

A common theme throughout the book is the warning signs that time and again were reasoned and explained away. The most striking example of this is seeing her colleagues hide losses the company was making in off balance sheet businesses. Essentially pushing losses into associated business so that they wouldn't have to be reported to the company's investors. This was a dubious practice but one that did take place legitimately if certain criteria were met. When Watkins questioned the practice initially, she was told that

---

[84] *Corporate Awards*, Enron Corporation. Available from https://enroncorp.com/corp/pressroom/awards/corporate.html [accessed December 2023].

[85] M. Swartz and S. Watkins, *Power Failure: The Inside Story of the Collapse of Enron* (2004).

this was too complex for her to understand (a common rebuff at Enron) and that she shouldn't worry, as the losses would be added back to Enron's balance sheet at a later date. This, she rationalized, was okay… as long as it was declared in due course.

Watkins was, however, very uneasy about it. She wanted to leave in the mid-1990s, but she had joined Enron at a lower position than she would have liked and hadn't yet secured a promotion. She felt this would reflect poorly on her CV and therefore stuck it out.

Leaving judgement of the rights and wrongs of the situation aside, we can probably somewhat understand her outlook at this point. As time went on she appeared to lower her standards as to what was acceptable behaviour. Even what was acceptable behaviour from other colleagues towards her. As the pressure mounted, Watkins was subjected to verbal abuse on many occasions by her boss Andy Fastow. Promotion was held out as a prize for those willing to lower their standards. The water was starting to boil.

Considering this situation, the question really comes down to our personal standards and where the boundaries are drawn. Let's look a little deeper.

The compromise of individual morals

Group values affecting personal values is something that has been seen time and again. And not just in the financial world.

A study reported in the 2011 *Personality and Social Psychology Bulletin*, involving 82 students of mixed genders from the Italian University of Chieti-Pescara, set out to establish how moral values shared by the ingroup affect the behaviour of individual group members.[86]

The study found that 'members were willing to let go of individual behaviour preferences to behave in ways approved by the group'. Certain moral behaviours, they found, were a source of group pride and ingroup identification, regardless of social status. Furthermore, consensus within

[86] S. Pagliaro, N. Ellemers and M. Barreto, 'Sharing moral values: anticipated ingroup respect as a determinant of adherence to morality-based (but not competence-based) group norms' in *Personality and Social Psychology Bulletin* 37 (8), (2011).

the ingroup about what's morally appropriate was decisive. Group members generally sought and obtained approval and respect from other group members by exhibiting actions in line with the ingroup consensus on moral behaviour.

In short, there's a gravitational pull towards what the group determines by consensus is appropriate moral behaviour.

As individuals entering workplace scenarios, for example, we must be conscious of this possible effect on our own behaviour, particularly over a longer period of time. Similar to the six phases of fraud we looked at in Chapter 8, group cultural corruption can be a gradual assault on 'the individual's personality structure and values'.[87] However, the options open to people in his situation may be limited.

Sherron Watkins' story epitomizes the gradual effect of Enron's deviant corporate culture. She experienced a growing awareness and moral conflict that ultimately led her to a crucial decision. That decision was to expose the wrongdoing despite the potential personal and professional risks.

This transformation highlights the profound impact that a corrupt corporate environment can have on individuals, particularly those with a strong ethical compass. Unfortunately, of course, not every bright and ambitious recruit at Enron had the strength to do what she did.

Clearly, the erosion of personal values in the face of group moral norms can be striking. But what about people who basically work for themselves, in jobs that have an unshakeable sense of moral direction, such as medical professionals?

Purdue Pharma

On 23 October 1996, Richard Sackler, CEO of Purdue Pharma, emailed senior executives within Purdue to confirm what they had suspected.[88]

---

[87] T. Cleff *et al.*, 'Motives behind white-collar crime: results of a quantitative and qualitative study in Germany' in *Society and Business Review* (2013).

[88] S. Chakradhar and C. Ross, *A history of OxyContin told through unsealed Purdue documents*, STAT (2019). Available from www.statnews.com/2019/12/03/oxycontin-history-told-through-purdue-pharma-documents/

'Physicians who attended the dinner programs or the weekend meetings wrote more than double the number of new Oxycontin prescriptions compared with those who did not attend.' The dinner programmes referred to in Sackler's email were events hosted by the pharmaceuticals company, which served as opportunities to 'hard-sell' to doctors. During these weekends, practising and prescribing doctors stayed at luxury hotels, enjoyed lavish meals and attended numerous presentations organized by their hosts, all expenses paid by the company. Does this sound familiar?

It turns out that the doctors were fed not only dinner, but also a barrage of skewed statistics and misinformation about Purdue's new 'wonder drug', Oxycontin, which Purdue claimed had a less than 1% addiction rate among patients. This was basically a lie. Oxycontin is, like all opiate painkillers, highly addictive and open to abuse as a street drug.

The doctors were intentionally misled so that they would prescribe more and more of the drug to their patients. And, for the most part, it worked. What resulted from these unscrupulous and fraudulent sales tactics was an out-of-control addiction crisis in the US that's arguably worse than any yet seen from prescription medication; the impacts are very much still being felt today.

Of course, like all corporate fraud, there were many players and many moving parts in this story: culpability is shared. However, in this case, while the blame may be shared, some are evidently owed a greater share than others. Purdue was the driving force of this crisis, without doubt.

The mystery

Nothing evidenced Purdue's malicious intent in starker terms than how they reacted to the strict drug prescription laws that were in effect across five states of the US – California, Idaho, Illinois, New York and Texas. These became known as Triplicate States. Focus groups organized by Purdue (prior to the launch of Oxycontin in 1996) with doctors across these US states resulted in some disturbing feedback. Doctors were anxious about prescribing opioids such as Oxycontin – this was clearly going to be a barrier to sales.

The doctors' anxiety stemmed from the oversights and regulations in place to govern opioid prescriptions. The Triplicate laws, as they were known, stated that any doctor prescribing drugs from a restricted list had to follow a strict procedure.[89] They had to use a state-issued triplicate form for these drugs, each with its own serial number. One copy would be retained in the doctor's office, one would be given to the patient and one sent to a federal government office, a drug monitoring agency. This was extremely effective as an accountability and monitoring measure. Purdue found that doctors in the states where these laws were in effect were much less inclined to prescribe these restricted drugs.

The fact that they had a filing cabinet full of prescription forms was a powerful reminder of how they were handling this sort of prescription medication. It was as basic as that. The doctors, as is human nature, simply felt they were being watched.

There was also a corresponding filing cabinet in a state office somewhere with their name on it; it would be easy to see if any doctor had a bulging file of restricted prescriptions and should perhaps be audited in terms of their prescribing practices. The oversight in Triplicate States was, it might be said, enough to bolster the personal value structures of those doctors in a way that effectively reminded them how dangerous opioid drugs potentially were.

But the really damning thing is how Purdue reacted to this information. Instead of listening to the concerns of the doctors in their focus group and changing the way they planned to market a highly addictive drug, Purdue instead decided to simply avoid marketing to doctors in the states where the Triplicate laws were in effect, focusing instead on those states without such effective checks and balances in place. In other words, focusing on where they had the potential to influence the doctors' individual ethical standards.

It's estimated that The Triplicate laws saved an estimated 25,000 lives in New York alone.[90]

Summary

The corrosive effect of morally rogue organizations on those within their orbit should not be underestimated.

---

[89] A Scheduled 2 Drug under the Controlled Substances Act (CSA) 1970.

[90] *Gladwell on Doctors' Prescription, Carbon Copies and the Opioid Crisis* – Cautionary Tales with Tim Harford 2022 Podcast.

Choosing the right people as opposed to just the right skill sets is an essential starting point. The culture we then expose these people to comes into focus and is of equal if not more importance. The lesson is simple: culture is everything. The Triplicate system demonstrates the benefit of building, nurturing and monitoring a framework to withstand the headwinds of rogue cultures in society.

Finally, leaders in any organization or group dynamic would always do well to remember that it's not just what we say, it's what we do… and what we condone.

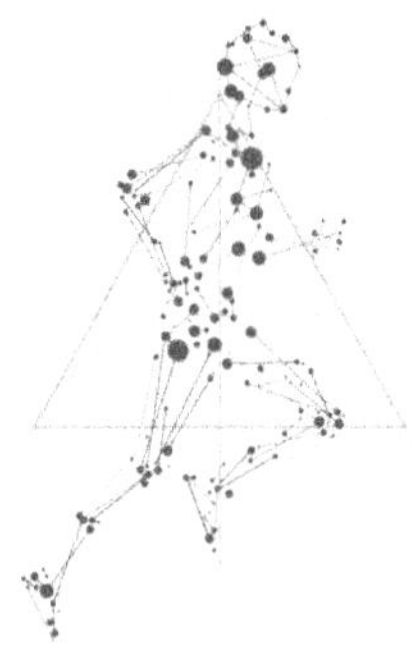

10
Moving the Needle

> 'Focus on the vital few, not the trivial many.'
>
> **Richard Koch**[91]

Imagine for a moment a five-year-old boy stumbling upon a relic of the past. This is a chess set from the 1940s, weathered by time and neglect. The set, a Christmas gift once bestowed upon this child's mother, who herself had never ventured into the world of kings, queens, rooks and knights.

This was Mark Quinn's first encounter with the game of chess.

His mother, lacking in chess knowledge but not in spirit, endeavoured to convey the essence of chess to her son. Her efforts, while fragmented, inadvertently cast a spell over Mark. A fantasy about knights and soldiers locked in a strategic battle upon a chessboard.

Mark's fascination with chess wasn't merely a child's fleeting interest but a spark ignited by a deeper, perhaps primal, yearning – a yearning for understanding, for mastery, for connection. This yearning drove him to implore his parents for guidance. Yet his parents' unfamiliarity with the game led instead to a reliance on a borrowed library book to instruct their eager son, propelling him on a destined path.

---

91 R. Koch, *The 80/20 Principle: The Secret to Achieving More with Less* (2022).

Not far from their home lay a further stepping stone: a chess club offering junior classes. This, combined with Mark's enrolment in Gonzaga College, Dublin – an institution on the cusp of establishing its own chess legacy – laid the groundwork for what would become a defining journey. A convergence of opportunity, interest and potential.

At this point something extraordinary happened.

At the age of 12 Mark had a chess FIDE rating of about 1,000. For context, a FIDE rating of 1,000 would be considered somewhat average to below average, perhaps for anyone who played regularly. But by the age of 14 he had a rating above 2,000, which by most people's estimation would be an expert-level rating, in the top five percentile globally.[92] It was a rating level that had brought him to the junior world championships in the US that year. How was this possible? Motivation is one thing; means and method are quite another.

In this chapter, we're going to examine what really moves the needle in terms of improvement.

Stick-to-it-ness

In the first part of this book we looked at many of the skills that can really make a difference to our success journey. In Part 2 we're now concerned with how we apply those skills (such as connecting with our 'Atomic Motivation' – Chapter 4) and ourselves to maximize positive outcomes.

Someone recently sent me an acronym of the word SUCCESS. Each letter represented a word; for example, the first S in Steady Leadership.[93] The second-to-last S: Stick-to-it-ness. I joked that they must have been stuck for an extra S at the end. Stick-to-it-ness sounds made up. This trait may, however, be the most important aspect of achieving positive results.

---

[92] See *Elo rating system*, Wikipedia, The Free Encyclopaedia (Last modified 10 April 2024). Available from https://en.wikipedia.org/wiki/Elo_rating_system

[93] G. Berge (@bg1121). Social Media platform X (Dec 2023). S–Steady Leadership, U–Unselfish Attitudes, C–Committed, C–Confidence is Earned, E–Energy Givers, S–Stick-to-it-ness and S–Strong Team Culture.

Professor Daniel F. Chambliss, who studied excellence in the field of swimming for many years, is of the opinion that natural ability and giftedness 'are generally used to mystify the essentially mundane process of achievement in sports, keeping us away from a realistic analysis of the actual factors' of excellence. He suggests in his book, *The Mundanity of Excellence*, that this misattribution of where these great results come from is actually preventing us 'from a sense of responsibility for our own outcomes'.[94]

Chambliss concluded, after years of studying athletes, that while talent certainly helps, particularly at the beginning, the gold medal usually goes to the person who has put in the most time and effort. As the title of his book suggests, excellence is mundane. It's repetition, refinement and endless practice that produces elite results. While this may sound depressing, it's actually really good news for the average person, because the playing field is more level than you think.

His point is that if we lazily view others' success as simply a giftedness that they received, and we did not, this essentially lets us off the hook from even trying. Why bother if success is predetermined? Why risk almost certain failure? If, however, we realize that extraordinary outcomes such as Olympic success are actually the result of consistent training and repetition, then the question changes from 'I can't… so why should I bother?' to 'why can't I?' Why *can't* you repeat, refine and put in endless practice in whatever field you choose? The answer is… of course you can. Generally, with *remarkable success*. And especially with the use of 'deliberate practice' methods, which we'll discuss in Chapter 11.

Returning to the puzzle of how Mark Quinn improved so much in two years from the age of 12 to 14, it's clear that he applied stick-to-it-ness.

I was quite a bit older than Mark when I started playing chess – aged 42 – and my strategy was to simply play five speed-chess games per day online after I learned the basics from my neighbour and local chess teacher Tony McMahon.

I can tell you this much – studying the game of chess is *boring*. It's tiring and difficult to read chess books. You typically need to have a chess board in

[94] D. Chambliss, *The Mundanity of Excellence: An Ethnographic Report on Stratification and Olympic Swimmers* (1989).

front of you to move the pieces as you read. It's a language all of its own. It's not too hard to find a basic opening to practise using YouTube videos, etc. (depending on how you learn best), but textbooks delve into potential responses and discussions around understanding the dynamics of different positions.

So, for example, the Ponziani is a basic enough chess opening for white but, once you're a few moves in, a textbook explanation can look like this: Nxe4 often continues 5.d5 Ne7. 5... Nb8 is also *playable*; Black even may invest a knight with 5... Bc5 6.dxc6 Bxf2+ 7.Ke2 Bb6 8.Qd5 Nf2 9.Rg1 0-0 10.cxb7 Bxb7 11.Qxb7 Qf6 12.Na3 e4 13.Nc4 Rab8 14.Qd5 exf3+ 15.gxf3 Rfe8+ 16.Kd2 Ne4+ 17.fxe4 Bxg1.[95]

You tend to need a bucket of cold water nearby to stick your head in after reading a few paragraphs… just to stay focused!

As a beginner, I found it difficult to escape the pointless feeling of studying abstract chess lines and variations, which may never come up in an actual game. Later, when I became a student of Mark Quinn, I changed my approach. I instead started to play fewer games and to focus more on reviewing past games I had played, together with a focus on chess tactics. To illustrate the point further, I once played an online game (which I won – humble brag) against an opponent who had played 48,972 games online. Their number of games played far outstripped my own – but I could see that their online chess 'ranking' wasn't high, around 950 on www.chess.com.

Let's consider an obvious question: if this person's goal was to improve at chess, was playing 48,972 games online the best use of their time? If we take it that these were mostly five-minute blitz games, using five minutes as a base calculation (many games may finish sooner), this could amount to as much as 240,000 minutes played, or 4,000 hours. Or two years' full-time working at something like 39 hours per week. We've heard so much in the media over years about how practising for 10,000 hours can make us an expert, so this person was almost halfway there. Or were they?[96]

Based on what I've learned from Mark, I don't think so. It became very clear to me that their time may have been focused more on the 'trivial many' in

---

[95] Wikipedia contributors, *Ponziani Opening*, Wikipedia (last modified 8 February 2024). Available from https://en.wikipedia.org/wiki/Ponziani_Opening

[96] The famous 10,000-hour rule – which we'll explore more in Chapter 11.

terms of games played, instead of the 'vital few' – namely, the study of chess strategy and tactics.

Trent Dyrsmid: one paperclip at a time

Trent Dyrsmid is a serial entrepreneur, known for his work in creating scalable business processes. Born in Vancouver, Canada, Dyrsmid is the founder of Flowster.app, a platform designed to automate workflow for companies. His career has been marked by his focus on process automation and efficiency. His image on social media strikes me as one of determination and readiness to delve into work.

Back in 1993 Dyrsmid was a rookie stockbroker. He had been hired, right out of college, by a firm based in Abbotsford, Vancouver. Most companies have relatively low expectations of what employees new to the workplace can accomplish, but within two years he had built the biggest customer book of business in the firm, worth over $5 million per annum. He had outperformed all of his colleagues, even though they all had more experience.

Management at the firm were intrigued; they wanted to know his secret.

His approach was simple, he explained: at the start of each day he had two jars on his desk, one filled with 120 paper clips and the other empty. Every time he 'cold called' a potential client, he moved a paper clip from the full jar into the empty jar. Here's the important bit: the paper clip got moved to the other jar regardless of whether or not a sale was made. The psychological reward of moving the paper clip was for making the call, for pitching the stock to a customer. It demonstrated, in a physical way, the progress he was making regarding the part of his objective that was within his control. The outcome of the call was not. The paper clips became a tool to track and artificially create momentum – a 'momentum tool'.

He had zoned in on the one thing that was most important in business: asking for the sale. Many of his colleagues would spend their workdays in activities *tangentially* related to asking for a sale, such as reading the news cycle or market reports, and using other methods to try to predict what stocks would perform. They made a fraction of the cold calls that Dyrsmid made. Why? Well, deep down, no one wants to be rejected, and being rejected call after call can be a pretty miserable experience.

But Dyrsmid didn't see it that way; he saw each call as progress. Regardless of a sale or rejection, each call took him one step closer to his goal of 120 paper clips. Failing to get the sale on one call or another wasn't really *failure*. The only failure was not making the call in the first place. He instead saw it as an opportunity to hone and refine his sales pitch. The physical act of moving the paper clip helped him develop a sense of forward momentum, perspective and reward.

In another arena, addictive social media apps have been designed with this psychology in mind. Many of these apps can waste our time, but one productive learning app called Duolingo uses this psychology very effectively. The app teaches languages and creates a streak when players use it every day. If the user misses a day, their streak, represented in a calendar on the app, returns to zero. In May 2023 Duolingo had over three million active daily users with streaks amounting to more than 365 days.[97]

It's a momentum tool with a twist, however, because if you miss a day you lose your investment of time (at least as represented on their app calendar). If we take a step back, this looks completely meaningless, a little like moving a paper clip every time we make a call, but our minds don't work logically in this way.

If we pause and think about this, the learning is that we can manipulate our minds into giving these trivial rewards more weight than their actual importance, thus enhancing the reward for our focus on the *vital few* activities that bring effective and sometimes rapid improvement. We can be creative about how we invent and use these momentum tools in order to find what works best for us. Just like reading a dull chess book can be a miserable experience, it all depends on your perspective.

Back when 12-year-old Mark Quinn was a mediocre chess player, he encountered Gerry Murphy, a teacher at his school who had a real interest in the game and encouraged the students to play. The all-important role model, which is a common theme in this book.

Very few students played chess in Mark's school class, but he described to me how this presented a challenge and an opportunity. It gave Mark players

---

[97] L. Von Ahn, 'How to make learning as addictive as social media.' TED Talk, May 2023.

to 'aim at, in the year ahead'. This meant he had to work hard to improve, because his rivals at the school were a year older and had an extra year of playing.

The school went on to win almost every chess competition they entered, including the Marlwood Tournament in England, a tournament for the best schools from across the UK and Ireland. Mark describes how being a good chess player was already very important to him and very much became wrapped up in his identity. Playing older players effectively helped push him out of his comfort zone (which we'll explore more in Chapter 11).

In his book, Professor Daniel F. Chambliss seems at times almost dismissive of talent.[98] So where does talent fit in the equation?

'Talent buys you a ticket to the party,' says Simon Pond, who spent 13 years as a professional baseball player and knows what it is to devote your life to a sport. When Simon and I spoke, we probed the question of where talent fits in the success journey of becoming a pro baseball player. At spring training each year there are about 200 ball players per organization, and 25 of these will make it to the major league roster. What separates the successful few from the rest tends to lie in competency.

Anyone, regardless of natural talent, can have a strong work ethic. Of the 200 ball players who have the bodies, coordination and natural ability, work ethic is what separates the best from the very best and creates the necessary competency. Creating competency means honing the body and mind through purposeful and engaged practice. Simon became one of those final 25 members of the major league roster in 2004.

To get a sense of the work involved, after Simon retired from the professional game he later played recreationally. One of his fellow players on his post-retirement amateur team, Gary Pennington, once told me he counted how many 'ground balls' (this was where a coach bats baseballs along the ground for the player to field with his glove) Simon took *before* training. Remember, this is post-retirement. For an amateur team. Playing recreationally. Gary counted 72 baseballs. That's a lot. This gives us some insight. Gary was a former professional and he was impressed.

---

[98] D. Chambliss, *The Mundanity of Excellence: An Ethnographic Report on Stratification and Olympic Swimmers* (1989).

It seems clear that Simon is someone who strongly connected with the rationale and importance of mundane practice, but did he have a 'momentum tool'?

Journalling was something that featured in Simon's toolkit of performance. Writing about pitches thrown at him, how training sessions went, filling each day of the diary with insights, learnings and progress.

That sounds like a 'momentum tool' to me.

Finding the next level

At 12 years old, something significant happened for Mark Quinn that inspired him to raise his chess game to an elite level. Up until this point, he had never actually studied the game and had played with what he describes as 'a beginner's mindset'. He had never played in a tournament outside of a school context, so when he was selected to attend a day-long event for talented school-age chess players, he ended up playing kids with much broader experience than his own. Some of the other kids had also already played chess internationally.

For Mark, the day ended in frustration and disappointment for two reasons. First, he didn't know how to record chess notation, which made solving chess puzzles (an important element of the day-long event) tricky. Most of the other kids seemed well versed in this skill. Second, during a simultaneous match, a type of chess match where one strong player plays several others at once, he was accused of cheating by moving a piece twice, as opposed to once, by the strong player who was conducting the simultaneous match. Feeling unjustly accused, Mark went home that day very upset by the experience. In fact, he describes being so upset that he decided he didn't need this level of stress in life, and it was touch and go whether he wanted to play again.

As it happened, his mother bumped into the organizer of the event about a week later. In a throwaway remark, the organizer said, 'Oh, yes, I remember Mark. He's far too immature ever to become a good chess player.' His mother reluctantly reported the conversation to Mark, who was so angered by the comment that it proved to be a huge turning point for him. He changed his approach, which up until then had mostly been playing chess and enjoying the game in its simplest form.

Moving the needle

Mark's new approach was to refocus his effort not on *playing* chess, but the study of chess. He essentially started doing something any of us can do: he spent endless hours on key aspects of practice that were much less enjoyable but drove much more improvement. For example, after some persistent requests, his parents bought him eight large encyclopaedia chess books, which he began to work steadily through. This was a daunting task, as there are over 1,300 possible chess openings alone, quite aside from the middle games, end games, tactics and puzzles that one might study.[99] It would be easy to spend a lifetime learning them all, and never master everything about the game.

With this new motivation, Mark got stuck in and started to memorize chess variations, read chess strategy books and work on the difficult activities that would dramatically improve his game.

In an age with no online chess or internet, using only chess books and his encyclopaedia, Mark began to play out games and puzzles on his chess board by himself. He asked his father to take him to the nearest chess club, which only had adult members, and he played each week on Thursday and Saturday evenings. He structured his learning in a way that distinctly separated his approach from the vast majority of his opponents. Or to phrase it another way, his inputs were very different. Essentially, Trent Dyrsmid and Mark Quinn had a lot in common. They both found ways to really move the needle in terms of performance, and importantly to note for the rest of us, these were activities that their competitors were *not willing* to do.

Champions ignore trivial enjoyable activities in favour of the tough but vital actions. The true differentiator is their stick-to-it-ness. This perhaps comes from reframing the activity in our mind in order to connect with the ongoing sense of progress (such as Dyrsmid moving a paper clip) or the meaning and motivation Mark Quinn found by leaning into a devastating insult and using it as fuel to plough through the hard work necessary to accelerate improvement. Proving people wrong can be a powerful tool and a life-changing 'why'. Mark

---

[99] *The Oxford Companion to Chess* by Oxford University Press lists 1,327 named openings and variants, and numerous others are in common usage to varying extents.

took that negative experience of the disastrous one-day event and used it to change his life.

He later went on to become an international chess master, and Ireland's number-one player at the age of 17.

Summary

For those seeking to replicate this sort of success we must understand the inputs, not just the outputs, and find the *way* to follow through.

In the next chapter, we'll examine how elite performers use their time effectively when tackling the *vital activities* they've identified.

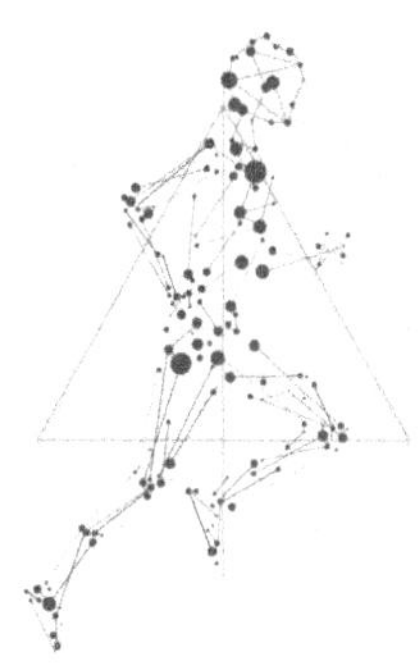

11 Balanced Brilliance

'He spoke of a dream…'

The year was 1963.

The sun bore down on Washington, DC, its rays beating upon the National Mall with an intensity that matched the passion of the quarter-million souls gathered there. It was a day of music and message, a symphony of voices rising in unison for a cause that pulsed at the heart of America.

Bob Dylan's chords wove through the air and mingled with the stirring harmonies of gospel singers, creating a mosaic of sound that enveloped a diverse assembly. Ten speakers, each a titan from the varied factions of the activist world, took their turns at the podium. Their words, imbued with the weight of struggle and the hope of change, echoed across a sea of listeners.

As the clock neared 4pm the anticipation was palpable. Hours had passed under the relentless sun, with temperatures soaring above 90°F. The crowd, united under a common banner, had weathered the heat, their resolve undimmed from early that morning. They stood at the precipice of a moment that promised to transcend the physical discomforts of the day.

Martin Luther King Jr took to the stage with a typed speech in his hand. This speech had the surprisingly uninspiring title of 'Normalcy Never Again'.

It had been laboured over and drafted carefully to tread a political middle ground, away from militant hardliners, reaching out to white allies, while at the same time responding appropriately to President Kennedy's civil rights bill. Every word was measured and weighted to the tight seven-minute time slot allocation.

His speech started powerfully with references to standing in the shadow of the symbolic Lincoln Memorial and the Emancipation Proclamation, which, he articulated, had become a broken promise. The US government had defaulted on its obligation to support the life, liberty and pursuit of happiness by people of colour.

Halfway through his speech, which aimed to bridge the chasms dividing a nation, Martin Luther King Jr found himself at a crossroads. He seemed to be faltering under the weight of the occasion's ambition. The words on the page, crafted to appeal to a broad spectrum of interests, now seemed awkward, almost at odds with the fervour and vibrancy of that historic day. It was a moment teetering on the edge of mediocrity.

But then the atmosphere shifted as a sentence emerged from King's lips. He read from the typed script powerful words partially quoting the bible – Amos 5:24: 'We will not be satisfied until justice rolls down like waters, and righteousness like a mighty stream.' This wasn't just rhetoric, it was a clarion call, resonating deeply with the gathered masses along the National Mall. A surge of approval rippled through the crowd. A tangible affirmation of King's vision.

Emboldened by this reaction, King faced a decision as his gaze returned to the scripted words before him. The next line seemed pale, hollow, even pretentious given the occasion. It was a divergence from the authenticity that the moment demanded. In a pivotal decision, King chose not to be shackled by the prepared text. He looked beyond it to the sea of faces before him, to the collective experience of struggle and hope that had brought them there – some directly from the confines of jail cells.

In search of words that could truly encapsulate their sacrifice and herald a future filled with promise, King was momentarily adrift in the enormity of the task. It was then that a voice cut through the uncertainty, a voice familiar with the power of lifting spirits through song. The gospel singer Mahalia Jackson spontaneously shouted, 'Tell them about the dream, Martin.'

This interjection, this moment of serendipity, spurred King to depart from his prepared remarks and navigate towards the shores of what would become his most enduring legacy.

It's difficult to exaggerate the risk King was taking by going off script at this point. The stakes were extraordinarily high. The pressure on Dr Martin Luther King Jr and other civil rights leaders to capitalize on this moment was immense, given the national and international attention it garnered. An event of this magnitude involved coordinating the transportation, accommodation and safety of hundreds of thousands of participants from across the country. The organizers had to plan the march's logistics without the benefit of modern communication technologies, relying on word of mouth, flyers and limited media coverage to mobilize participants.

This was a moment, the final speech of the day, that had to work. A misplaced word or phrase could strike the wrong tone or even alienate potential allies or insult current activist partners.

King delivered.

He spoke of a dream, a vision that transcended the immediate struggles and painted a picture of a future defined by equality, justice and harmony. This impromptu deviation wasn't just a departure from a pre-written speech, it was an alignment with destiny, a testament to the power of authenticity and a reminder of the transformative potential of speaking from the heart.

The heat, the sweat, the hours on their feet faded into the background as King told of a dream. A dream that would reverberate through time, long after the last notes of the day's music had faded away. The words of this dream were so perfectly unscripted and powerfully orated that it shook America to its core on the national airwaves and became one of the most iconic speeches of all time. In many ways it was a high-water mark in the articulation of what a global success objective should be, to live on this planet together in peace, embracing and celebrating our racial and cultural diversity.

It was a moment King seized with both hands and triumphed with brilliant improvisation, which brings us to the subject of this chapter. What we witnessed that day was, viewed through another lens, the application of a carefully refined and cultivated skill. A skill applied in a broad and powerfully impactful way, which transcended the occasion and struck a righteous blow against the negative and miscued dogma of racism. A blow that, with the power of timing and a live media supercharge, would become immortalized for all time in a world struggling generation after generation for a touchstone of what it means to be human.

But, this wasn't just some off-the-cuff solo run by King. He had in his possession little known (or at the time understood) tools, developed to capitalize on a moment of great opportunity. He had a method to his brilliance, as do all elite performers.

In this chapter, we ask the question not just of how the structured development of expertise can be achieved to maximize its positive impact when the moment arises, but the choice of that acquired brilliance. A cost-benefit analysis, so to speak, of the time it takes to refine and develop a skill, tallied on the weighing scales of potential application. We'll return to this subject and Dr King later in this chapter.

Part 2 of the book centres on how we apply skills and ourselves to take on and overcome challenges. In this context, I set up a coaching and education business in 2022 called askmore.ie. This name appealed to me because we could all do with asking a little more from ourselves and, in turn, more from life. The general advice tends to be 'try harder' and 'work smarter'. In the information world we can now benefit from an ocean of knowledge at our fingertips. We can connect knowledge and approach challenges in new and informed ways. But the starting point is to challenge ourselves.

Challenge

We learn from an early age that if we want things, the magic word is 'please'. Recent science, however, tells us that if you want to ask for something lasting and important, such as a stronger body or more brain power to solve problems and meet challenges, the magic word isn't please – it's 'homeostasis'.

Homeostasis is our body's internal balancing system, which we can use as a tool to improve at things by asking it to rebalance to a new normal. For example, homeostasis in the context of physical fitness refers to the body's ability to maintain internal stability while adapting to physical stress or changes in the external environment. When exercising, the body undergoes various changes (e.g. increased heart rate, respiration and metabolic rate) to meet the increased demand for energy and oxygen. The process of homeostasis works to return the body to its baseline state post-exercise, ensuring that internal conditions remain stable despite external changes.

Over time, with regular physical training, the body's homeostatic controls become more efficient, improving fitness levels and the body's ability to handle more intense or prolonged physical activities. The body calls for more resources to meet the new demands. This adaptation is a cornerstone of physical fitness improvement, as it enhances endurance, strength and overall performance.[100] In this context, we must push our body to show it what we do not have and what we need to obtain, forcing that adaptation.

Let's take a moment here to consider this point. How many push-ups or chin-ups do think you can do? This might be a challenge someone threw down when you were ten years old, such as how long can you hold your breath for? How many numerical digits can you remember if someone calls them out to you, one per second? Pause to have a think about these things for a moment in order to gauge your current perspective on your depth of ability or resources.

If we look at what's possible with training at the extremes of human ability, verified world records for those activities are figures such as 10,507 push-ups in one session (by Minoru Yoshida of Japan) or 7,479 chin-ups in 24 hours (by Graham Morgan of the UK). Kate Winslet, the actress, developed an ability to hold her breath for an amazing 7 minutes 15 seconds while training for the movie *Avatar 2*. Even more amazing was the fact that Winslet reported that she only had three weeks of training in order to accomplish such a feat. The world record for this is in fact a lung-busting 24 minutes 37 seconds, a record set in 2021 by Budimir Šobat of Croatia.

Obviously, these are the extremes of human endeavour and they generally involve lifelong dedication, but they illustrate the important point of... *what is possible.*

---

[100] For more on homeostasis, see S. Libretti and Y. Puckett. *Physiology, homeostasis*, NCBI Bookshelf. Available from www.ncbi.nlm.nih.gov/books/NBK559138/ [accessed February 2024].

Enhancement of skill

So once we've identified key things to focus on as discussed in Chapter 10, how can we then best spend our time on those *vital few* things in order to improve rapidly? Let's return to the example of the young Mark Quinn, the chess International Master, who featured in Chapter 10.

Between the ages of 12 and 14, Mark went from an average chess ranking to expert level. I interviewed him to find out how we can classify this extraordinary improvement and perhaps replicate it for us mere mortals.

Again, Anders Ericsson in his very impressive book, *Peak*, articulates two types of practice that, through carefully detailed research, have been proven time and time again by elite athletes to work.[101] These are deliberate practice and purposeful practice.

The question in my mind was which was it that Mark Quinn employed at 12 years, if either?

Ericsson's hypothesis is that there's a key difference between deliberate and purposeful practice in enhancing performance. Deliberate practice, he states, is essential for achieving high-level expertise and involves structured, focused activities with specific improvement goals, demanding attention and effort. The key to deliberate practice (as opposed to purposeful practice) is the presence of a strong coach who can facilitate a critical, constructive and timely feedback loop to the student in order to identify gaps and correct mistakes. The coach will develop targeted drills after reflecting on performance gaps, which will allow refinement and focused repetition. Finally, these drills and exercises will be incrementally increased in difficulty to keep the student in the learning zone, just beyond their comfort zone, by establishing difficult but manageable objectives – perhaps just above their current skill level.

This rigorous targeting of performance is not inherently enjoyable. In contrast, purposeful practice has all the same ingredients without the benefit of a strong coach. As such, it may be a little less intense (depending on the motivation of the student) and, therefore, in my experience, just a little bit more enjoyable, yet still effective for general skill enhancement.

[101] A. Ericsson, *Peak: Secrets from the New Science of Expertise* (2016).

In summary, deliberate practice is the key to mastery and expertise, while purposeful practice suffices for general skill improvement and perhaps accommodates more enjoyment.

I spoke with Mark Quinn regarding his approach. Around 1990, when Mark began to practise intensely, there was a lot less knowledge around about how to develop expertise. Mark didn't have a coach. His local club simply played games, and they didn't teach him anything in particular, he recalls. In addition, his school also didn't provide chess coaching. In fact, it wasn't until he was 15 years old and had a chess rating of well above 2,000 that he received any real coaching. This practice would fall into the self-taught training of purposeful practice as opposed to deliberate practice.

Mark, it's clear to me, has a structured and disciplined mind that enabled him to clinically set out goals and adapt his intense practice in accordance with measurable targets, which provided him with timely feedback.

This demonstrates that thousands of hours, even without a coach, can bring us to expert level, using purposeful practice; for example, gaining a FIDE chess rating of over 2,000 – somewhere in the top 5% in the chess world.[102]

But, perhaps to go all the way to Grand Master or even world chess champion, we need that extra push from a world-class coach with knowledge of deliberate practice principles and to have the ability to endure being pushed to our limits. For me, it makes Mark Quinn's achievement no less remarkable.

He's not the only one, of course, who took these initial steps themselves without the benefit of focused coaching. Simon Pond, the former Major League Baseball player who also featured in Chapter 10, told me that from the age of ten he got out of bed every morning and swung a baseball bat 200 times. Here's the important bit: he didn't just swing the bat, he watched his body shape in the large window in his bedroom to allow focus on the correct hip through the ball swing motion and other nuances, allowing immediate feedback and the necessary correction. This sounds familiar. Interestingly, he stated that he would get up in the middle of the night and swing the bat even years later in the professional minor leagues. In fact, he thinks that, in his 13-year professional career, he never met anyone who had swung a baseball bat as much as he did in his life. He was among the thousands or maybe millions

[102] https://maroonchess.com/is-chess-rating-2000-good/

of other ten-year-olds over the decades who wanted to fulfil sporting dreams such as hitting a home run at the historic and iconic Fenway Park, Boston, as a Major League Baseball player. What he did about it from that age made all the difference… he actually made that dream happen.

Remarkable things and moments years in the making

Martin Luther King Jr's 'I have a dream' speech had a significant tangible impact on American society in the 1960s. It galvanized momentum for the civil rights movement, influencing public opinion and leading to concrete legislative changes. The speech played a role in the passage of landmark civil rights legislation, including the Civil Rights Act 1964 and the Voting Rights Act 1965, which aimed to eliminate racial discrimination and ensure voting rights. Additionally, it inspired a generation to advocate for equality, fostering a cultural shift towards greater racial integration and social justice in the United States.

Outside America it contributed to the civil rights causes and activism in places closer to home, such as in Northern Ireland. The Northern Ireland Civil Rights Association, formed on 9 April 1967, aimed to address systemic discrimination against Catholics regarding the allocation of public housing, employment and other issues regarding the Catholic minority at the time. This period marked the beginning of a significant civil rights movement in Northern Ireland, which sought to address and rectify the systemic inequalities and discriminatory practices.

Even further afield, the speech's positive ramifications were voiced on posters in Tiananmen Square, China, in 1989. It still echoes around the world today in the #blacklivesmatter movement and in war-torn places such the Middle East, where someone wrote on a wall built by Israel in the West Bank: 'I have a dream. This is not part of that dream.'[103]

But a lesser-known fact is that, on 28 August 1963, Martin Luther King Jr capitalized on years of preparation and hard work. In the previous 12 months alone he gave hundreds of speeches on closely related topics. He was

---

[103] G. Younge, *The Speech: The Story Behind Dr. Martin Luther King Jr.'s Dream* (2013).

even well known for spending up to 15 hours of preparation for sermons each week at his local Baptist church in Atlanta, Georgia. He was meticulous in his preparation.

Since King was a small child he had been steeped in speech-making and oratorical skills. He was born into a family deeply rooted in the Baptist tradition. His father, Martin Luther King Sr, was a prominent Baptist minister. This environment exposed young Martin to religious discourse and the art of preaching from an early age. King was an avid learner. He attended Morehouse College, where he studied sociology and became involved in public speaking and debate activities. He then went on to Crozer Theological Seminary, where he deepened his theological knowledge and refined his preaching skills. His education continued at Boston University, where he earned a doctorate in Systematic Theology. Throughout his education, King was exposed to various oratory styles and philosophical thoughts that influenced his own speaking style.

Additionally, King's father and other preachers of the time influenced his oratorical style. As King grew into his teenage years, his skills were honed through continuous practice and active engagement in public speaking, with the benefit of real-time feedback from his audiences.

King's oratory and preaching skills were the product of a multifaceted and dynamic interplay of his background, education, influences and personal qualities, all underpinned by continuous practice and a deep commitment to his cause.

But it was his departure from his typed speech in 1963 and his impromptu 'I have a dream' finish, spoken from the heart, that changed everything. It's hard to see the 'normalcy never again' of the original text inspiring people to the same degree. Interestingly, this was also something that King had practice in, and under pressure.

Eight years earlier he was swiftly appointed president of the newly formed Montgomery Improvement Association to help coordinate a boycott in Montgomery, Alabama, following Rosa Parks' arrest for refusing to give up her seat on a bus on 5 December 1955. He had little time to execute his usual meticulous preparation and was forced to instead gauge the mood at Holt Street Baptist Church, which was filled to capacity, with additional crowds outside listening to the speech through loudspeakers.

He largely met the challenge by reading the response of those in attendance as they stamped their feet on the floor of the church in approval, finding unscripted inspirational words as the speech progressed. In a similar way, he would read the audience reaction years later in Washington DC.

So King definitely had real-time practice of going off-script, together with a close feedback loop; that is, the reaction of the audience as he developed and perfected his skill over the years. He had practised the 'I have a dream' speech, or versions of it, so often in the previous 12 months that his speech advisor, Wyatt Tee Walker, told him, 'It's a cliché, you've used it too many times already.'[104] King had used the speech several times in the months leading up to August 1963, including well-attended rallies in Detroit and Chicago. In fact, his aides had heard it so often that Walker's reaction when King broke from the typed script was: 'Aw shit, he's using the dream.'[105]

To understand the backdrop and preparation of the speech is in no way intended to take away from the magic of what King achieved under enormous pressure. The point is to bring that magic a little closer to our grasp and understand to a greater degree what's possible with focused practice.

Good enough

Returning to the concept of the 10,000 hours needed to become an expert, this can be incredibly off-putting for people. We must also bear in mind that success in one area of your life may often mean failure in other areas, whether it's relationships, social skills or even general health.

The good news is that if we adjust our thinking and instead evaluate the potential *application* of these proposed new skills, we can change things positively and quickly. For me, training to break the world record for chin-ups or holding my breath doesn't have a whole lot of application in my life.

Now, if we love doing something, like Mark Quinn did, it's a wonderful thing to be able to keep up such an activity, central to your life journey. To Martin Luther King Jr the application was, of course, to spread God's word; a life

---

[104] Ibid. See Introduction: 'Lightning in a Bottle'.

[105] Ibid.

vocation for many. It ended up being a tool and skill that changed the world when the opportunity presented itself.

He, of course, is an exceptional example of developing a key core skill that ultimately made him a history-maker and a force for positive change in the world. But setting out on this journey we may be much better served developing a range of skills, particularly when skills may complement each other.

The figure of 10,000 hours reduces to something in the region of 20 hours of focused practice to get to a level of basic competence. This focused practice should, for maximum results, use the metrics we've discussed in terms of purposeful or deliberate practice, allowing timely feedback and the ability to push yourself.

You can learn to play the guitar, sing, write, dance… whatever. You'll be astounded at how good you become in those initial 20 hours of hard effort. This information is liberating and we can pick and choose the skills to acquire. For example, the writer Jose Kauman has an interesting TEDx talk and book on this subject called *The First 20 Hours, How to Learn Anything… Fast.*[106]

Some of the greatest business leaders, such as Indra Nooyi, exhibit a wide range of skills, both technical and soft, which are crucial to effective leadership. She was widely regarded for her networking prowess, connecting with global leaders and influencing PepsiCo's strategic partnerships. As the former CEO and chairperson of PepsiCo, one of the largest food and beverage companies globally, she demonstrated exceptional leadership and a diverse set of skills that significantly contributed to the company's success. But it wasn't just one core skill she developed, such as public speaking, it was a wide range of diverse skills, many of which complemented each other.

The challenge for you, the reader, is to select, develop and couple complementary skills to effectively overcome challenges. Although we have little information on how many hours Nooyi spent polishing her skills, we can develop basic competencies quickly with practice and guidance, particularly in the area of communication. These skills are *not* something that we need thousands of hours to become reasonably good at, in my opinion.

---

[106] J. Kaufman, *The First 20 Hours: How to Learn Anything… Fast* (2013).

Other factors of course weigh in. If you're introverted and would prefer to develop other skills on your journey, that's your choice, but the choice is there. The bottom line is that we're masters of our own destiny. It's simply a matter of balancing our perspective and applying ourselves to the type of brilliance or good enough that gets us where we want to go.

A final word of warning to parents and mentors. Just because we can't see the immediate application of a skill or pursuit that our child or student loves to do, be cautious about dismissing its application. A case in point is that of a student who told a teacher that they wanted to become a 'YouTuber' when they grew up. The suggestion was dismissed as 'not a real job'. Be gentle with criticism and supportive in outlook.

Summary

Brilliance is a choice. Balancing it refers to bringing perspective to that choice. Sometimes, however, the answer is simple: 'I love doing it,' and it suits my 'ticket to the party' – as discussed in Chapter 10.

Whether it begins with a child's fascination, stirred by finding a discarded chess set, or the awe of watching your father deliver an inspiring Baptist church speech. Staying with that… could just be enough to change the world.

12
Balanced Stress: The Engine Room of Performance

> 'Do not let your work consume you; remember to make time for yourself. Too much work dulls the blade, and too much play leaves the field untilled.'
>
> **Greek poet Hēsíodos**[107]

The tennis player Mardy Fish embodies the tenacity of a relentless competitor on the court. From the outset, his journey may have seemed ordinary, just like any other player climbing the ranks. But hidden beneath the surface was a motivation and willingness to push himself to the limits of human experience.

As described in Chapter 4, a pivotal moment took place late in his career at a lesser-known tennis tournament in New England, when a lacklustre performance left him floundering in defeat. Amid the disappointment of his performance, given the relentless hard work he had put in over the previous six months, something inside him snapped. He unleashed a new-found aggression, slapping himself on the face and later screaming at his

[107] Hēsíodos was an ancient Greek poet generally thought to have been active between 750 and 650 BC, around the same time as Homer.

opponent, actions never seen before in the laid-back player. This sudden eruption of inner fire would forever alter the trajectory of his career. The metamorphosis was nothing short of extraordinary. He went on a meteoric rise through the tennis rankings from 123 to 7 in the world in just two years, leaving opponents bewildered as he relentlessly pursued victory. He defied the norms of tennis players who rarely experience a late-career performance transformation of epic proportions.

His desire to prove himself as a world-class tennis player had long become an intrinsic part of his identity. By the end of 2011 he had successfully fulfilled his ambition to secure a spot in the prestigious Barclays ATP World Tour Final, a season-ending competition that sees only the top eight players in the world compete, and he was the number one-ranked tennis player in the US for the first time.

In the midst of this remarkable surge, however, Mardy Fish's journey encountered an unexpected and formidable adversary: the limits of his own body and mind. Just as he seemed poised to reach new heights in his career, fate dealt a devastating blow. Cardiac arrhythmia and a crippling anxiety disorder emerged. As his anxiety escalated, it manifested in debilitating panic attacks, leaving him grappling with paralysing fear. The mere thought of facing Roger Federer, one of tennis's giants, in a crucial quarter-final match at the 2012 US Open triggered a torrent of distress. The boundless potential that once propelled him forward now teetered on the brink of implosion. He had crossed the thin line between triumph and defeat before even entering the first game against Federer, forfeiting the match and ultimately everything that he had invested in.

But why? Why did his career unravel when other elite athletes surged forward? Delving deeper into his journey offers a fascinating exploration of the interplay between resilience and vulnerability.

In this chapter, we'll explore:

1. Where can the balance be struck between all-out effort to improve and sustaining well-being?
2. Did Mardy Fish just ask too much of himself in terms of improvement or was there a way he could have achieved a form of balance, sustaining his elite performance, built on a solid foundation of well-being?

Stress and performance

While stress is usually seen as a negative force, linked to burnout, heart problems and ultimately a shorter lifespan, let's consider an alternative view. What if Mardy Fish's remarkable growth and progress wasn't limited by stress, but rather propelled by it? His tennis accomplishments reveal a tale of human resilience but also a key obstacle on the path to greatness. Chronic stress, without a strategic recovery plan, simply leads to exhaustion and breakdown.

Our body's autonomic nervous system (ANS) regulates stress and recovery. The ANS handles vital functions such as digestion, heart rate and breathing, and consists of two subsystems: the sympathetic and parasympathetic systems. The former triggers our fight or flight stress response, while the latter oversees our rest and digestion mode. There's a natural equilibrium between these systems that our body oscillates between. Importantly, lifestyle changes, illness or unexpected events can disrupt this balance, numbing our stress state's responsiveness and pushing us into survival mode unknowingly. This often leads to anxiety, illness and eventual burnout.

In a world where stress seems like an antagonist, it should perhaps be regarded more as a catalyst for growth when coupled with a strategic recovery plan. Mardy Fish's journey exemplifies this proposition, reminding us that the human spirit thrives not by evading stress but by managing it wisely. The balance between exertion and replenishment takes centre stage, offering a fresh outlook on how we can reach our zenith while nurturing our well-being.

First, let's delve a little deeper into his situation in order to understand how unchecked stress can overwhelm even the brightest and best of us.

Identity

In the intricate web of tennis culture, where prodigious talents emerge and thrive, Mardy Fish's story, at its core, is a narrative about identity, conditioning, pressure and a formidable adversary: mental health.

Imagine a two-year-old child, skilfully volleying tennis balls over a net on a sunlit court. This wasn't any child, it was Mardy Fish, and the court belonged to his father, a professional tennis coach. That scene, captured by a Minneapolis TV station, set the stage for a life where the boundary between the person and the athlete blurred until they were one. Tennis wasn't just a sport for Mardy Fish, it was an identity.

From personal experience and to take a business example, there's a moment in the careers of certain lawyers where a subtle shift occurs. The office walls seem to close in, just a little. The name on the door, once a badge of independence and achievement, becomes a shackle. It's a story not about law per se, but about the perils of conflating identity and occupation. Regulations tighten like a noose, profits are squeezed, yet leaving the profession seems inconceivable. This is more than a job, it's an identity. The crux here isn't that the lawyer is committed or passionate – those are admirable traits. The danger lies in the fusion of vocation and selfhood into a single, brittle identity.

It's a cautionary tale and valuable insight for all of us, regardless of profession. Pour your heart and soul into what you do, absolutely. But let's not forget that being a committed professional is not the same as being a hostage to your career. There should always be a space, however small, that allows for the possibility of retreat, recalibration or even reinvention. We should maintain a *balanced* perspective that allows us to manoeuvre when the landscape changes, as it invariably will.

So, as we contemplate the plight of our hypothetical lawyer, this isn't a warning to avoid commitment; it's a reminder to keep a small part of ourselves in reserve. It's that sliver of detachment that can prevent a fulfilling career from becoming an inescapable trap.

In the world of tennis, as Mardy Fish grew, so did the expectations surrounding him. At 15 he found himself in the manicured courts of Saddlebrook Tennis Academy, a world away from home. Here, young talents were not just trained in tennis but were moulded and chiselled into stoic warriors. Coaches at Saddlebrook believed that kids, teeming with raw emotions, lacked the steely resolve of a champion. Hence, the ritual of twice-weekly mental toughness videos: 'No whining. No complaining. No escape routes.' This was the doctrine, paired with depictions of what 'weakness' looked like. The subtext? Emotions are a luxury, an impediment to success.

But Saddlebrook was just one chapter. Post-academy, his life took another twist. He found himself under the same roof as the budding superstar, Andy Roddick. Living with the Roddicks was akin to training in a tennis boot camp, with Andy's father, Jerry, a stern disciplinarian with a military background, at the helm. Every day, every action was a testament to discipline and dedication.

The early 2000s was a tumultuous period for US tennis. After basking in the golden glow of legends such as Sampras, Connors, McEnroe, Agassi and Courier, a lull had settled. The hopes of a nation, the pressure of filling those colossal shoes, weighed on both Fish and Roddick. Pressure mounted as Fish was dispatched along the conveyor belt of talent, held firmly by the gravity of self-identity as a tennis pro and muted by the pressure cooker of a macho culture with no room for showing weakness, such as sharing emotions.

Yet, for Fish, the most relentless pressure came from within.

2012

After reaching number seven in the world in late 2011, the 2012 season offered him lots of new opportunities. His relentless pursuit of greatness had meant huge sacrifices. He had practically stopped socializing, as he found solace in his new-found competitive edge. The appearance fees were now much higher, and he had an opportunity to play in new tournaments he had never been invited to before. He and his team therefore decided to pack his schedule. Australia, back to LA for six days, flying to Switzerland for a Davis Cup match, back to LA for four days, on and on it went. It was non-stop. It became more 'difficult to switch off', noted Fish around this time, and his energy started to flag. He started to take Ambien (which treats insomnia) to help with the time zone shifts. 'Objectively I was doing well… I wish I was able to tell myself that,' he said in an interview in 2012. But all Fish could focus on was doing better, giving himself little credit for his achievements.[108] Doesn't this all sound a little strange? He and his team don't seem to have planned for rest and recovery periods.

Things started to unravel at a Miami tournament in May 2012 where he performed poorly. Immediately after the game he heard his Davis Cup

---

[108] Charting our progress is not just a nice thing to do. It's essential to our continued growth and motivation. Giving ourselves credit, celebrating wins and taking time to be grateful. Research has shown that there are myriad physical and psychological benefits to spending time in the positive state of gratitude. See Fredrickson *et al.* (2000) and Fredrickson & Levenson (1998). See also *The Psychology of Gratitude* by Robert A. Emmons & Michael E. McCullough (2004).

captain Patrick McEnroe describe his performance as horrendous on national television. This hit hard. That night he suffered a tachycardia event, which is a physical misfiring of the electrons in the heart. After surgery to resolve the issue he began to be afflicted by anxious thoughts for the first time, which just wouldn't go away. This led to less sleep, more worry and so on. By the time the US Open took place in late August, his world ranking had slipped to 23.

Loss of balance

At the 2012 US Open, Fish engaged in a long, heart-pounding late-night duel against Gilles Simon, just prior to the quarter-final fixture with Roger Federer. Fish saw off Simon in a hard-fought battle, not just against an opponent but his own fatigue in a game that didn't end until the early hours of the morning. The consequence? An exhaustion of the little fuel he had left in the tank, allowing negative and intrusive thoughts finally to enter his one safe place, the performance arena. A burnout that wasn't just physical, but mental, the effects of which he still confronts even today.

Let's reflect on this situation for a moment: the telltale indicators were lurking in plain sight, quietly heralding the impending storm. A fresh and palpable ferocity had materialized on the court, an uncharted facet that quickly became indispensable to his playing style. This transformation wasn't without its sacrifices; the ceaseless grind of training dispensed, for example, with leisurely social time. The weight of soaring expectations also bore down. His very sense of self became fragile and intertwined with his performance as a tennis player. It all hung in the balance.

Amid this whirlwind there was also an unrelenting travel schedule, which began to take its toll. Moments of respite grew scarce and recovery periods dwindled. The chorus of critique, even from the most trusted circles, began to resonate as his performance faltered. And as if the symphony of challenges wasn't complete, there was also the stoic norm of a macho tennis culture to be observed. It became a suppression of inner turmoil for him, concealed behind a thin façade.

It all could have perhaps… been so different.

In the world of elite performance, a crucial yet often overlooked factor looms large: the weight of life's demands and pressures. Experts have coined a term for this collective burden: 'life load'. Dr Ken Van Someren, a respected authority in the field, points out an intriguing paradox.[109] Our bodies, marvellous in their adaptability, generally thrive under increased stress. But there's a catch: our bodies can't differentiate between beneficial stress that propels us towards peak performance and other negative stressors. Regarding Mardy Fish, factors such as extensive travel, disrupted sleep, amplified media scrutiny and criticism from fans and friends had all multiplied in intensity, sending his *life load* through the roof.

Certainly, external stressors played a significant role, but lurking within this intricate cause-and-effect chain an anxiety disorder had also begun to take root in Fish.

Recent advances in heart rate measurement have unveiled valuable insights into our body's responses to stress. In simple terms, when the heart rate exhibits a steady beat-to-beat variation, it indicates that the body is under duress. Conversely, varying heart rate timings suggest that the body is in recovery or rest mode. It seems the heart's electrical function maintains a steady rhythm when tackling problems. This field of study is known as heart rate variability (HRV). While HRV analysis remains a realm of ongoing exploration and we have a lot more to learn, it promises valuable insights into restorative activities and our body's resilience.

I had the privilege of speaking with Harvard professor David Eddie, who shed light on this exciting intersection of technology, science and high-performance sports. Professor Eddie noted that individuals grappling with underlying conditions such as anxiety disorders have diminished capacity to adapt and cope with stressors. Mardy Fish found himself ensnared in the perfect storm – a cocktail of stress that grew overwhelmingly potent.

But what if things could have unfolded differently? Both experts concur that the human body isn't a mechanical device. You can't plug it into a linear training programme and expect guaranteed positive outcomes. Instead, we must navigate a middle ground that balances many interests. Success must be built upon a foundation of a healthy body, mind and emotional state. The

---

[109] Dr Van Someren is a world-leading expert in human performance, working for over 25 years with many of the world's greatest sports champions. He was Director of Sport Sciences at the English Institute of Sport, leading the support of Great Britain's athletes to their historic medal haul at the London 2012 Olympics. See https://kvsperformance.co.uk/about-us

latter, in particular, has perhaps been undervalued, with family and friends playing a crucial supporting role.

When it comes to resilience, HRV technology offers key insights into our body's ability to shift from stress to recovery – a measure of our resilience fitness, akin to a fit person swiftly recovering from a run. Two intriguing frontiers emerge:

1. HRV technology allows people, for the first time, to identify activities that genuinely contribute to their goals – such as writing, reading or engaging with others who are highly restorative in nature. These activities, once viewed as stressors, are now seen as productive avenues for rejuvenation. Personally, I've found such activities, especially creative and engaging tasks like writing, to be particularly restorative, often immersing me so deeply that I lose track of time. Autonomy in completing these tasks further enhances their restorative power.

2. Dr Van Someren likens these restorative activities to plugging in a smart phone. While smart phone batteries tend to degrade over time, our body's batteries can, in fact, grow and expand. This expansion is often a result of enduring significant stress while experiencing quality, deep physical, mental and emotional recovery. For many successful athletes, leaders and business people, such growth can be traced back to childhood experiences involving trauma, such as bereavement or parental separation. Some emerge from these experiences broken, while others benefit from the support of family, enabling them to rebuild and increase their resilience. The key, it seems, lies in subjecting the body and mind to stress and then following it with profound physical, mental and emotional rejuvenation.

One final piece of the Mardy Fish puzzle was the timing of his last match in the 2012 US Open. We now have a great understanding of how our chrono type threatens our sleep in a 24-hour cycle.[110]

Summary

Stress isn't the villainous force we ought to banish from our lives. In fact, it plays a pivotal role in propelling us towards greatness precisely when we

[110] Chrono type is the propensity for the individual to sleep at a particular time during a 24-hour period.

need to deliver our best. Picture it as the driving force, the unseen hand urging us to perform at our peak. But – and there's always a 'but' in these tales of equilibrium – we must tread the delicate path of balance. It's the art of measuring our efforts with precision and coupling them with a thoughtful recovery strategy.

Of course, it's possible to ride the stress train too hard, pushing ourselves past the point of no return. When we subject our bodies and minds to relentless overtraining and unyielding strain, we can trigger a phenomenon known as 'maladaptation'. It's like the body and mind's way of raising the white flag, conceding defeat in the face of relentless pressure.

But – and here's where the magic lies – in the right hands stress can be a formidable ally. With an astute approach we can summon extraordinary effort while keeping ourselves relatively safe from the pitfalls of excess. It's all about tapping into our evolving understanding of how our bodies interpret stress, not merely during the sweaty grind of training and performance but also in the grand tapestry of life, where we're entangled in the intricate web of external expectations and internal pressures.

In essence, we ought to be diligent students of the stumbles and missteps of those who have walked this path before us. Let's not be too proud to seek the wisdom of others and to embrace the guidance available to us. The key lies in constructing a sturdy foundation of well-being upon which we can build performance. In essence, it's not about vanquishing stress but about mastering it, understanding its rhythms and using it as a potent force.

Part 3
Congruence

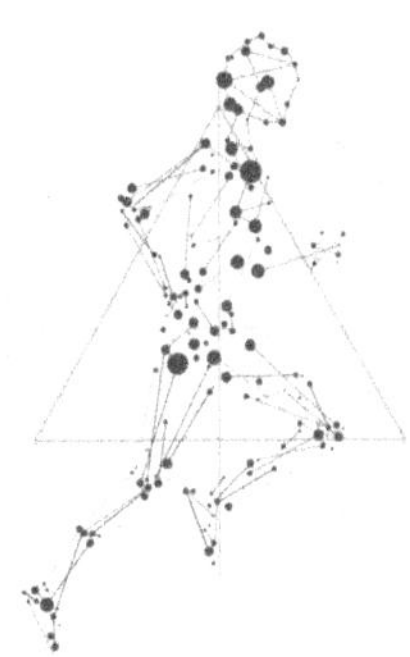

13 Control

Confucianism: imposing responsibilities on ourselves or others without considering autonomy and well-being is not in line with a harmonious society.[111]

On the afternoon of 9 April 2017, United Flight F3411 sat at O'Hare Airport, Chicago, fully occupied and ready to depart. The passengers settled into their seats with a ceremony most of us are very familiar with. As luggage was stowed and seatbelts fastened, they were about to experience what could be described as one of the most infamous mishaps in corporate history. What would happen in the next 20 minutes would cost the airline an estimated $140 million-plus in legal settlement costs, and wipe approximately 4% – $1 *billion* – off United Airlines' share value.

An announcement was made shortly after boarding that four seats were needed for United Airlines staff. Volunteers were requested to depart the aircraft. Passengers were initially offered an incentive of $400 in travel vouchers, a hotel stay and a seat on a flight leaving the next day. When no

[111] J. Tiwald, 'Ren, Li, and their Relation to Values and Individual Autonomy' in *Stanford Encyclopedia of Philosophy*, edited by E. Zalta (last modified 15 July 2019). Available from https://plato.stanford.edu/entries/ethics-chinese/#RenLiRelValConValIndAut

volunteers emerged, the voucher portion of the offer was increased to $800. According to passenger Tyler Bridges, an airline supervisor then walked on to the plane and brusquely announced, 'We have United employees that need to fly to Louisville tonight… this flight's not leaving until four people get off.' The manner of this announcement, he recalls, just 'rubbed some people the wrong way'.[112]

Just before 5.40pm (the scheduled time for departure), a new announcement boomed over the aircraft's comms system. Four passengers would be selected by computer and asked to leave the plane. At this stage a level of anxiety rippled through the packed aircraft. The metrics of the computer program used to select the passengers included the price paid for the flight, frequent flyer miles accumulated with United Airlines and other binary metrics.[113]

Three of the passengers who were informed about their selection, although annoyed, complied and left the plane. The fourth selected person was Dr David Dao, a 69-year-old Vietnamese-American passenger. Under pressure to see patients at his clinic the following morning in Louisiana, he refused to depart. By all accounts, Dr Dao was polite but firm in his dealings with airline staff. Nevertheless, the airline staff persisted and requested assistance from the Chicago Department of Aviation Security.

Faced with unyielding security staff, Dr Dao did what many of us might not think to do: he called the airline on his phone and began to explain his situation. Dr Dao explained that he was hosting a medical clinic for war veterans the following morning. Information that one might expect to matter in terms of negotiating with a US airline: a doctor, needing to attend a medical clinic, for a very noble and patriotic cause. However, none of these metrics were programmed into the computer selection criteria. When the phone call ended, the officials threatened him with force and ultimately jail if he didn't voluntarily leave the aircraft. He again politely refused. The two officers wrestled him out into the aisle of the plane, his head colliding with the seat rest in the process. Dr Dao suffered a broken nose, lost two teeth and was dragged in humiliating fashion off the plane.

---

[112] A. Selk, *The Washington Post*, 10 April 2017.

[113] J. Gunter, *United Airlines incident: what went wrong?* (10 April 2017). Available from www.bbc.co.uk/news/world-us-canada-39556910

The result: days spent in hospital by Dr Dao, suffering from concussion and injuries incurred, plus a PR and financial disaster for the airline. How could this happen? The answer is that strange, unpredictable and often dangerous things happen when we place responsibility on people but remove their autonomy.

In this chapter, we'll examine the harmful effects of a lack of control or a perceived lack of control, for both individuals and organizations, and why it should be an important individual goal to move towards more autonomy in our lives.

Health havoc: the consequences of autonomy deprivation

The relentless pursuit of efficiency and profit, regardless of the toll it exacts, manifests itself in diverse ways, often intertwined with distinct cultural trends. Take, for instance, China's notorious '996 culture', a term that encapsulates a working existence extending from 9am to 9pm, six days a week. Beyond the glaring issue of these unsustainable and life-consuming hours lies a deeper problem: the nature of the work undertaken within this punishing framework further exacerbates the predicament, robbing workers of not only their autonomy but also their well-being. Mounted upon the mundane, highly pressured and closely monitored nature of this work, businesses find ways to informally exert pressure on staff to clock these 72-hour-plus working weeks.

Business leaders such as CEO Jack Ma, who rose from poverty to become one of China's richest men, is one of the most fervent supporters of 996 culture, calling the hectic schedule a 'huge blessing' for young professionals. 'If you find a job you like, the 996 problem does not exist,' he states.[114]

Let's pause here: isn't Mr Ma missing a key factor in his assessment of the situation? Many of these jobs are difficult to like, let alone be truly passionate about. As we delved into in Part 1, motivation serves as a pivotal element in the recipe for success at anything. Yet, within the motivational cocktail, passion emerges as a vital ingredient, fuelled by the fertile grounds of creativity. In the

---

[114] K. Gilchrist, *Alibaba founder Jack Ma says working overtime is a 'huge blessing'* (15 April 2019). Available from www.cnbc.com/2019/04/15/alibabas-jack-ma-working-overtime-is-a-huge-blessing.html

employment sphere, creativity is nurtured through relationships built on trust. However, it's essential to recognize that all these elements hinge upon a healthy level of autonomy and empowerment. Sadly, in the relentless pursuit of profits, autonomy and empowerment, once-valued attributes of successful businesses, are becoming increasingly scarce commodities.

Revenge bedtime procrastination and the unexpected symptoms of overwork

In an article entitled 'Obedience and fear: the brutal working conditions behind China's tech boom', the *Financial Times* in June 2021 reported that businesses such as Alibaba (which employs more than 250,000 staff and had grossed just under $110 billion dollars in that same year) impose competitive ranking assessments on staff.[115] These rankings are a zero-sum approach, where those not working as hard as their peers are weeded out and expected to leave the business. The article describes workers queuing for buses home at 10.30pm, with many staff members still working.

In fact, a new phenomenon known in China as *bàofùxìng áoyè*, or revenge bedtime procrastination, has developed. It's essentially a personal rebellion against stifling control and long hours of work. This occurs when staff members arrive home and feel the need to reclaim personal time by staying up late, in many cases until the early hours of the morning, to watch movies, speak with friends and essentially experience an environment in which they're in control. As a result of *bàofùxìng áoyè*, many overworked employees aren't getting the seven to nine hours of sleep a night that's recommended for adults. Sleep deprivation in turn leads to all sorts of negative health consequences, including: difficulty controlling impulses, which leads to unhealthy habits such as smoking or a poor diet; a greater risk of accidents; depression; lower immune system function; and ultimately reduced life expectancy. The 996 culture is literally shortening lifespans.

A lack of control has been consistently linked to negative health outcomes in various research studies.[116] This perception can lead to increased stress,

---

[115] Y. Yang, *Obedience and fear: the brutal working conditions behind China's tech boom* (9 June 2021). Available from www.ft.com

[116] S. Robinson and M. Lachman, *Perceived Control and Behaviour Change: A Personalized Approach* (2016).

which in turn may exacerbate or contribute to health problems such as cardiovascular disease, weakened immune function and mental health disorders. Chronic stress associated with feeling out of control can lead to hormonal imbalances and inflammation, both of which are risk factors for a wide range of health issues.

Michael Marmot's book, *Status Syndrome*, is a compelling and worthwhile read that explores the relationship between social status and health outcomes.[117] Marmont argues that socio-economic position is a crucial determinant of health, even after controlling for income, education and traditional risk factors such as smoking. He introduces the concept of the 'status syndrome' to describe how one's perceived position in social hierarchies can impact the likelihood of suffering from various health issues, including heart disease, stroke, cancer and infectious diseases, and even affect rates of suicide and homicide. Marmot makes a robust argument that factors such as working in a highly controlled, low-autonomy environment are associated with poorer health outcomes. Outcomes that can lead individuals into a state of continuous crisis, triggering physiological changes that can contribute to diseases such as heart disease.

Anger and fear

In 2021, a whistleblower at Meta, Frances Haugen, revealed that their algorithms, particularly those used by Facebook, were designed to maximize user engagement, and in doing so they often exploited strong emotional reactions. The algorithms prioritize content that's likely to generate engagement, which often corresponds to material that elicits strong emotional responses from users. Why? More screen time by users, means more advertising revenue.

Our attention has become a commodity for a trillion-dollar business empire. The exact effectiveness of each emotion can of course vary based on the context and audience, but numerous studies and observations in the realm of social media psychology indicate that anger and fear can lead to higher levels of engagement. This phenomenon is often attributed to the fact that

---

[117] M. Marmot, *Status Syndrome: How Your Place on the Social Gradient Directly Affects Your Health* (2015).

such emotions prompt users to take action, such as sharing a post to express solidarity or commenting to counter an opposing viewpoint.

A study by Yale University, examining 12.7 million tweets, found that expressions of moral outrage are amplified on social media because such expressions receive more likes and shares. This reinforcement encourages users to express outrage more frequently over time, particularly among politically moderate users, who are more influenced by social feedback rewards.[118]

Let's unpack this a little. It's in the financial interests of some of the largest businesses in the world to grab our attention and precious time. Furthermore, this is most effectively done by making us angry, upset and afraid. If our working lives are becoming longer due to technology and the inability to shut off from work, and our personal lives are being consumed more and more by big tech algorithms specifically designed to make us angry and scared, this is a problem. It's a problem because control is ebbing away and less control strongly correlates to reduced health and well-being.

The detrimental impact of autonomy deprivation on society and achievement

These insights plainly underscore a concerning reality: prolonged work hours, the persistent perception of disposability and low status collectively wield a corrosive influence. These factors are essentially agents of health deterioration, disrupters of family harmony and eroders of self-worth. The consequence? A discernible decline in both individual and societal well-being, culminating in diminished public health outcomes and a curtailed lifespan.

What lessons can we draw from this when contemplating the path to success? It's fair to say that it firmly underscores the relevance of autonomy, and the cultivation of a robust internal locus of control, as the first of the following key things we should consider moving towards in our lives. Let's look at how we might take steps to achieve this.

---

[118] B. Hathaway, *'Likes' and 'Shares' teach people to express more outrage online*, Yale News (13 August 2021). Available from https://news.yale.edu/2021/08/13/likes-and-shares-teach-people-express-more-outrage-online

Learn to say no

There are some things we must do in order to maintain our income streams but there are always discretionary things that we can say no to. Saying yes of course feels good! It generally pleases others and leaves us feeling positive about an interaction. We feel competent and valued; we might even feel special or unique if we've been chosen to carry out a task or provide a service. But there can be too much of a good thing: saying yes too often can lead to burnout, resentment, let-down, overwork – the list goes on. The good news is that there's a true and liberating power in the word no. Far from being purely negative, 'no' helps us to develop and maintain boundaries, reduce stress, protect our productivity levels and, most of all, it establishes control and autonomy.

At times, we're all guilty perhaps of overestimating our ability to carry out tasks well, with energy and commitment. Narrowing our focus can significantly increase the quality of what we do. Try an experiment today: say no to something. This can be simply pushing something in your diary out to another date, or telling someone you simply haven't the bandwidth to do what they're requesting. If you're stuck for ideas, try this with the one object that consumes a lot of our time and energy: our smartphones. Instead of letting this device ride roughshod over your time and energy, use your phone instead to *reclaim* time. Cancel, reschedule, respond to requests with a polite… no! Feel the levels of stress reduce as the message is delivered. Finally, one great way to celebrate the space you've created for yourself is to diary in the request you've said no to, and when you open the app or your hard-copy diary for the day you were supposed to do whatever the request was, savour the feeling of autonomy you've created.

Create space

Loss of control has become a much wider issue in society. A stifling environment of control in the 996 culture or in bureaucratized large airlines stifles the space for talent and potential to develop. It seems more likely that those with ambition and creativity will seek to avoid or extract themselves from these suffocating environments. Perhaps we should instead start thinking about what responsibility we can delegate to those we mentor.

Nelson Mandela was incarcerated in one of the most oppressive and brutal prisons in South Africa in the 1960s. Everything about his life was controlled. What he ate, what he wore, when he would wake in the morning. Every aspect you can think of, even down to how he was expected to speak to the prison warders. Interestingly, he and his fellow inmates managed to maintain strong levels of well-being for reasons we'll explore in greater depth in our next chapter. One factor he speaks about in his book that also helped his well-being was the permission he was finally given to dig out a small garden. After ten years of requests the prison granted him permission in 1976 to start a garden. He speaks about the sense of control this provided: 'A garden was one of the few things in prison that one could control… this small patch of earth offered a taste of freedom.'[119]

Do not underestimate the power of giving 'a small patch of earth' to help sustain and invigorate those we mentor.

Responsibility, divorced from autonomy

Returning to the damaging effects of control in within organizations, how did this United Airlines incident escalate so dramatically? We might find a clue in an interview with another passenger, John Klaassen: 'After the first offer was made, the United employee left and it escalated… had they just tried some diplomacy, none of this had to take place… they were unwilling to negotiate.'[120] But is that really true? Could it be that the predicament at hand was rooted in a reluctance on the part of the staff to negotiate? Unlikely. The problem lay in the stark absence of discretion afforded to the airline's local staff, rendering them impotent in their efforts to engage in negotiation. In essence, a corporate predilection for a one-size-fits-all approach to complex scenarios that demand the delicate art of judgement had siphoned away the oxygen of common sense from the equation.

In the rush to maximize profits, there has been a trend for big corporate organizations, in particular, to systematically reduce autonomy at all levels of business. In the push to maximize efficiency, decision-making becomes

[119] N. Mandela, *Long Walk to Freedom: The Autobiography of Nelson Mandela* (1994), 582–583.

[120] *Sandy, Will you fly United Airlines again? Dragged Vietnamese man witnesses asked in CNN interview* (30 July 2017), via YouTube.

sanitized and regulated at a granular level – but the side effect is that power and responsibility become divorced. In the case of United Airlines, the local staff at O'Hare Airport had a lot of responsibility in terms of the safety of its 78 passengers, but very little autonomy, or power, to allow them to fulfil that responsibility. Where there's a mismatch in these two factors, significant problems can occur. There was no local manager who could go on to the plane to reason with a passenger, perhaps offering them alternative options or perks, or in the case of Dr Dao an obvious and merited exemption to the selection algorithm. Unable to apply any sort of nuanced approach to this volatile situation, the local United Airlines staff simply left it to security to remove Dr Dao, and the situation escalated badly. The apparent cost savings to the business of getting the plane in the air as soon as possible resulted in an inadequate one-size-fits-all approach instead of a dynamic approach to a complicated and unique situation. United Airlines aren't alone in this faulty thinking. As corporations push for efficiency, they can visit all sorts of negative effects on staff, their health and their families.

Summary

A move towards more control in our lives isn't merely about work-life balance, it's about the fundamental fabric of our well-being. A shift towards embracing more autonomy – not just in our jobs but in our personal lives – could be the linchpin in nurturing healthier, more resilient communities. It might begin with the seemingly small act of reclaiming control over the little things, which leads to a profound transformation in how we relate, mentor and thrive.

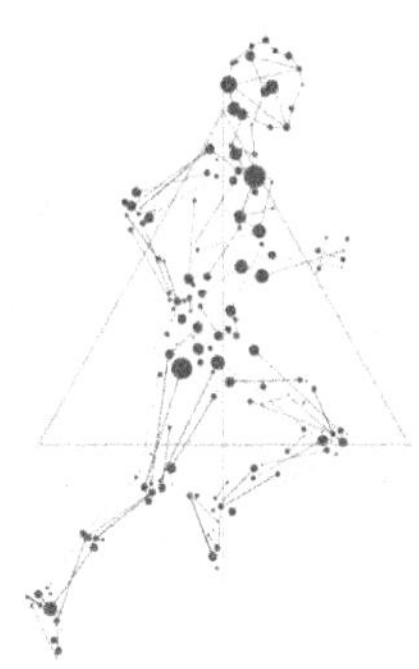

14 Purpose

> 'The heart of human excellence often begins to beat when you discover a pursuit that absorbs you, frees you, challenges you, or gives you a sense of meaning.'[121]

Imagine a cold windswept Irish beach in February 2024. We're on an army base close by, putting some elite athletes through a tough training session. In fact, the same training new army recruits will go through at this base in just a few weeks' time. These athletes are the Ladies Senior County Monaghan Gaelic football team. For those who know that sport, it's at a level somewhere between amateur and professional in recent years. These players are currently going through army hell. Press-ups. Burpees. Running with heaving army training equipment filled with sand and a stretcher carrying a would-be wounded soldier – a straw dummy in army uniform. All to the background sound of army drill instructors testing their mental capacity, challenging their competence and decision-making at every turn. You get the picture.

Then suddenly, as we approach the beach, running with the heavy and cumbersome equipment, Commandant Barber yells, 'Stop!' He then asks

---

[121] Dr T. Orlick, Professor in Sport and Performance Psychology at the University of Ottawa (22 June 2017). Available from www.success.com/17-inspiring-quotes-to-help-you-live-a-life-of-purpose/

a critical question: 'Do we want to put down any of the equipment?' The answer comes quickly from the one-day soldiers: 'No!'

I'm present with other coaches to observe and support the training exercises. When they start running again, I venture over and ask, 'If they had said yes, would you have let them?' The answer is very insightful. 'It depends on the response.' he says. 'Are they genuinely re-evaluating the situation, looking to the terrain ahead, assessing the prospect of injury to troops and other factors? If so, then probably… yes.' This is important. They're training decision-making and particularly the ability to re-evaluate as a fundamental military skill. As we'll see just a few pages ahead, it's also a fundamental life skill.

This is a sports team, however, not a military unit. As such, prior to entering the freezing waters to link arm in arm and suffer together as a team, he asks another perhaps more important question: why are we competing in a sport together as a team? Answers come but don't quite hit the mark. Commandant Barber continues. 'We have lost friends this year.' Life is short. 'We are doing this to accomplish something together, to make memories with this group of people. We may never have a chance to do the same with this particular group of people again.' He connects an overarching purpose to it all.

In this chapter, we're going to explore the importance of establishing more purpose in our lives. We're going to see how it can propel us forward, even extend our lives, not only in length but also in breadth and depth. We're also going to discover how establishing and mastering purpose can even help us manipulate our sense of time in a positive way.

Propelled by purpose

Moving towards and developing purpose can have a dramatic effect on motivation, not only for individuals but for groups of individuals. In Daniel Pink's book *Drive* he explores the concept of 'purpose maximization'.[122] It's a concept involving the establishment of group goals. Goals that supercharge effort in a group of people by tapping into a yearning to participate in something larger than ourselves. Something beyond personal gain.

---

[122] D. Pink, *Drive: The Surprising Truth About What Motivates Us* (2009).

In a business context this can sometimes mean establishing the contribution an individual employee is making to wider society, through our work. For example, an insurance business might connect their employees' work activity with the opportunity to help those in the local community to protect their homes, businesses and family income through insurance cover. In order to distinguish the reasons why being a client of our business is better than being a client of another, competitor business. Things all businesses should think about. With this thought process, profitability becomes incidental; that is, not the goal itself. Profitability happens on the way to achieving a broader goal of retaining existing customers and signing new ones, for the benefit of that customer.

In sports, teams can be galvanized and supercharged by a meaning that transcends sport. Commandant Barber used the powerful example of making memories with a group of fellow players, something we might not have a chance to do again. Achieving something worthwhile together.

Staying with the example of Gaelic football, in 2005 County Tyrone won the All-Ireland Senior Men's Championship. The highest accolade in Gaelic football. It was only the second time that they had achieved this, winning their first title in 2003. Cormac McAnallen, a player who had captained that team, tragically died in his sleep in March 2004 from an undetected heart condition. At just 24 years of age, it was a death that shocked the nation. It's difficult to exaggerate what an outstanding role model he was, as a captain, teammate and person. As a player he had achieved about as much as it was possible to achieve in his short life. His death had a devastating impact on the team in 2004. He had been named captain of the Tyrone senior team for the first time, just a few months before his untimely death, taking over from legendary 2003 All-Ireland winning captain Peter Canavan. In his first meeting with the team as captain prior to the start of the league, the team met at Quinn's Corner restaurant and guesthouse just outside Dungannon, County Tyrone. A player present at the gathering, and future footballer of the year, Sean Cavanagh, recalled when I spoke to him how Cormac stood up and, as part of a powerful and motivational speech, said, 'I won't accept a Tyrone team only known for winning one All-Ireland title.'

It was a difficult time for the team, and this was about much more than football. But those words stayed with the team as they took it upon themselves to make sure that he had belonged to a group winning two more titles, in 2005 and

2008. His memory wasn't used in some cheap way to motivate players, but rather it was a respectful and balanced approach, bringing friends together to do something worthwhile. After a season playing like men possessed, Tyrone won the 2005 All-Ireland title and dedicated it to his lasting memory.

Propose: long and healthy lives

Former South African President Nelson Mandela was aged 44 when he began what would be 27 years in prison. Two years later he was transferred to Robben Island prison, just north of Cape Town, where he spent the next 18 years in a damp concrete cell measuring 8 feet (2.4 m) by 7 feet (2.1 m), with a straw mat on which to sleep.

Mandela endured severe hardships during his imprisonment on Robben Island. Typically, the prisoners spent around eight hours a day, five days a week, engaging in 'hard labour'. In Mandela's case this involved breaking and moving limestone rocks, which was physically demanding and took a significant toll on his health. The heat was relentless and the bright reflections from the intense sun on the limestone caused permanent damage to Mandela's eyesight. The apartheid system's racial discrimination was evident even in prison. The black inmates received few privileges and inadequate food. Ultimately, this led to Mandela contracting tuberculosis. His contact with the outside world was also severely restricted, limiting his communication with family and supporters.

When he was released in 1990 at the age of 71, he was, however, in stable health despite damage to his lungs and eyesight from hard labour in prison. Mandela's post-release actions and demeanour show that he maintained strong mental health, enabling him to lead his country through a critical period of transition and become a global symbol of resilience and reconciliation, living a vibrant and active life until his death at the age of 95.

To put this in perspective, life expectancy in the black community in South Africa when he was imprisoned was somewhere in the mid-50s. Lower for those in prison. If he had just been living a normal life outside of prison, he might have been expected to live on average for just another nine or ten years. He was incarcerated for the next 27 years and subjected to brutal prison conditions and hard labour.

Let's take a moment to appreciate this point. This is remarkable in many ways. He was incarcerated by a brutal and racist regime that more or less locked him up and threw away the key. In his autobiography, *Long Walk to Freedom*, he describes the prison as it was in the mid-1960s: 'Robben Island was without question the harshest, most iron-fisted outpost in the South African penal system.'[123]

How was it possible for him to maintain such good physical and mental health? A clue perhaps lies in the policies of the apartheid regime. They didn't want Mandela and other high-profile anti-apartheid political prisoners mixing with the general prison population so they locked them up together at Robben Island. At this time, all the prisoners were black and all the prison guards were white. They punished them with hard labour and other measures.

To draw an analogy, the military does something similar with new recruits. Why? In order to galvanize them as a unit. Commandant Barber explained to me that 'we need to make the new military recruits experience hardship to help them form a bond, by seeing us as the enemy' – the drill instructors. An enemy they must face together. This is exactly what happened on Robben Island.

Mandela describes how he and his fellow inmates would keep morale up by singing while they worked in the lime quarry. He also talks about the opportunity he saw to unite with other anti-apartheid movements in the prison. 'The moment I arrived on the island, I had made it my mission to seek out accommodation with our rivals in the struggle… I saw Robben Island as an opportunity to patch up the long and often bitter differences.'[124] These were other political factions of the anti-apartheid movement who had, in fact, expressed disappointment that Mandela and others weren't sentenced to death at their trial in 1964.

He speaks in his autobiography of beginning to win a host of small battles with the prison authorities regarding prisoners getting their own uniforms in prison – long trousers instead of shorts. Significantly, he also recounts receiving the news of the deaths of his mother and, shortly afterwards, his eldest son. The authorities refused to allow him to attend their funerals. In a

[123] N. Mandela, *Long Walk to Freedom: The Autobiography of Nelson Mandela* (1994), 459.

[124] Ibid. See Chapter 5.

moving example of his bond with fellow inmates, he tells of the despair of receiving a telegram of his son's death: 'I returned to my cell not able to speak to anyone due to the grief.' Eventually, Walter Sisulu, a key leader in the anti-apartheid movement, was prompted by the other prisoners to find out what was wrong. He visited Mandela's cell. Mandela describes the interaction in a way to clearly show the emotional support they all provided to each other: Walter 'knelt beside my bed and I handed him the telegram, he said nothing, but only held my hand. I did not know how long he remained with me.'[125]

Research strongly supports the well-being power of 'community'. A study undertaken by Dr Stewart Wolf of the University of Oklahoma exemplified the well-being power of community found in a town called Roseto in Pennsylvania, US. This town defied medical logic in the 1950s.[126] Their levels of heart attacks and other illnesses were almost half the national average in the US. The study concluded, having ruled out all other known possibilities, that the sheer power of community spirit and togetherness was the source of these health benefits. Roseto, a town of just a few thousand people, had around 22 active community organizations. Many families had three generations living under the one roof and eating meals together. It was a town with an unusually close-knit social fabric. People would stop to talk to each other; they supported and interacted closely with one another.

The result: healthy and long lives despite average levels of exercise and relatively poor dietary habits. This sounds familiar.

Back on Robben Island there was one other key thing: Nelson Mandela's purpose. He had been a committed anti-apartheid movement member since 1943. Despite the harsh conditions and the personal sacrifices, his dedication to the anti-apartheid movement remained unshaken. He had suffered for a reason: equality and justice for a country of 48 million people. While in prison he became a symbol of resistance, and his refusal to compromise his principles for personal freedom was evident when he rejected conditional offers of release prior to 1990.

On a final note, Bill Clinton once recounted that he asked Mandela how he had put some of his tormentors in his government in 1994, when he was

---

125 Ibid.

126 See B. Egolf *et al.*, 'The Roseto effect: a 50-year comparison of mortality rates' in *American Journal of Public Health* (August 1992).

elected president. His reply was insightful: 'If I lived with hate in my heart, I could never truly be free.'[127]

Re-evaluation of purpose

Returning to the question asked by Commandant Barber, running with his one-day soldiers towards the beach. What he was looking for was their ability to stop and look ahead. Adjust and re-evaluate.

I recently interviewed a friend of mine for a podcast regarding purpose – Marcus Magee. Marcus at the time of the interview was in his early 40s and he described to me the perception of time flying by over the years. We've all had this experience. Our childhood up to ten years old can seem like it lasts forever. Our teens are slow but perhaps don't seem quite as slow. In our 20s time starts to speed up.

Marcus paused for a moment and recounted one exception. When he was 25 years old he took a two-year trip around the world to places such as South America – Brazil, Argentina, Peru, Bolivia, Chile and Paraguay. He then went to Fiji, New Zealand, Australia, Thailand, Cambodia, Vietnam and Laos. He met his future wife, a Dane who was also backpacking in Thailand. 'Those two years seemed like five years in terms of development and experience,' he recalled. 'After my 28th birthday, the next ten years just flew by.' He moved back to Ireland, launched an outdoor adventure business and started a family with his wife. 'That period of time went by in a flash,' he chuckles.

21 October 2021

Then a bombshell hit. He was diagnosed with cancer. This was devastating news. The initial symptoms he had experienced were put down to surgery the previous year for appendicitis, or perhaps Covid-19 symptoms, which had the country in its grip at that time.

He had surgery to remove a tumour just a few weeks later in November 2021. Unfortunately, this didn't halt the cancer's progress. At first stage one, then stages two and three. Finally, stage four cancer. This was scary.

---

[127] BBC Newsnight, *Bill Clinton on Nelson Mandela*, YouTube video, 12:01 (posted December 2013). Available from www.youtube.com/watch?v=JSG_31U6ab4

To step back for a moment: we've looked at how purpose can bring together and motivate individuals and teams of people, how a broader purpose can build community resilience and have dramatic and unexpected health benefits. But what if there wasn't much time left?

A remarkable study called the 'The effects of emotional states and traits on time perception' by Lehockey and colleagues investigated how personality traits, specifically the behavioural inhibition system (BIS) and the behavioural activation system (BAS), influence the perception of time.[128] BIS in action, for example, is when a person hesitates or refrains from making a decision or taking an action due to the fear of potential negative consequences. On the other hand, BAS is linked to the pursuit of rewards, positive outcomes and novel experiences regardless of or at least with a substantially reduced emphasis upon negative outcomes. Individuals who exhibit higher BAS scores tend to overestimate the duration of positive stimuli. While it can be dangerous to draw broad conclusions from these studies, it provides some basis for the fact that those adopting a positive outgoing mindset appear to engage more actively with positive stimuli. Changing our approach appears possible, the study indicates. While our BIS and BAS traits are somewhat influenced by genetics, they're also shaped by experiences and learning. Thus, with effort and practice, individuals can develop traits or behaviours that are more characteristic of BAS, even if they're naturally more inclined towards BIS. For example, the research indicates that if someone, adopting such an attitude, spent time in natural pleasant surroundings, they may be more likely to perceive time stretching, in turn perhaps making experiences more profound and memorable.

The theory is that novelty can knock us out of 'autopilot', so to speak. Our brains love autopilot. It's efficient, so we don't have to use much brain power. As we approach middle-age we work hard to get a secure place to live and raise a family. We surround ourselves with familiarity and routine. Contrary to that, new situations such as travelling, meeting new people and activities such as acquiring new skills, force our brain to churn through more information – making more memories.

---

[128] K. Lehockey *et al.*, *The effects of emotional states and traits on time perception*, East Carolina University (20 August 2018). Available from https://thescholarship.ecu.edu/handle/10342/7900

In a TEDx talk by Jedidiah Jenkins, he describes being in a car crash, and how time seemed to slow down.[129] He remembers listening to the song on the radio and thinking how bizarre it was that he was going to die listening to this beautiful song. He equates this time slowing down perception to when he travelled solo to South America on a bicycle for a 16-month adventure. He travelled, met new people, heard new languages, ate new foods… fell off his bike, etc. When he came home he couldn't believe the time perception difference. His friends, living their everyday lives, felt that he had been gone no time at all. He felt that he had lived many years of experience in those 16 months.

Why is any of this important? It's important because we can consciously live broad, deep and rich lives any time we want. We can force our brains out of autopilot into 'experience'. We can do this through meditation and mindfulness practice but also through challenge and a rediscovery of everyday life. Everyday life that we may perhaps think we know and have nothing new to learn from. To live this way we only have to look at how a child sees the world. The wonder and awe of a frosty morning, the night sky… the living world we can reach out and be a part of. Henry David Thoreau, a prominent American philosopher, naturalist and author, is well known for his reflections on the natural world, particularly in his book: 'I went to the woods because I wished to live deliberately, to front only the essential facts of life, and see if I could not learn what it had to teach, and not, when I came to die, discover that I had not lived.'[130]

Marcus was forced to reflect on his life and the reality that he might die at an age when his kids were, sadly, too young to even remember him. Looking to the metaphorical terrain ahead, he decided to change direction. He was also a talented musician. He temporarily closed his business and decided that music was an experience that would not only challenge, enrich and deepen the time left but also provide a gift and legacy he could leave behind. He had discovered a strong purpose.

As it happened, in the 1940s, two decades after Ireland had attained independence from the UK, the Irish government started a programme

---

[129] J. Jenkins, *How to slow down the passing of time*, TEDxOccidentalCollege. YouTube. Available from www.youtube.com/watch?v=70VIfWRdA-Y

[130] H. Thoreau, *Walden: or Life in the Woods* (1854).

to protect its heritage. It tasked primary school children to go out into the communities and gather old stories, poems and songs. These were written down and stored in numerous national archives. Marcus decided that the songs should live again for new generations. This was something he had wanted to do for years but could never find the time. With the help of a local historian, Hugh Barney O'Brien, he found a song about his hometown: 'Sweet Cootehill Town'.[131] It was a song last recorded as sung in County Clare in the early 1900s at what was termed an 'American Wake', which was basically a send-off party for those emigrating to the US. It had survived in music sessions along the west coast of Ireland afterwards, but was lost to the area it referred to: Cootehill, County Cavan. It was thought that the song was originally written around the 1850s.

Marcus became energized by this purpose and began researching and, where needed, writing the music for these old songs in order to breathe life back into them. He put a band together and started to perform these songs to sell-out shows. Thankfully his health began to stabilize and he has now recorded his first album.

Art and music certainly remind us of the beauty at our fingertips. Lost perhaps to those, particularly me at times, too busy to see it. Maybe it's a matter of taking the time to see that beauty and to force ourselves into the reality of the moment just a little more.

Another example of this is the famous impressionist painter Monet, who arrived in Venice by train on 1 October 1908 and was quoted as saying Venice 'is too beautiful to be painted! It is untranslatable!' Monet took four years to finish the painting *San Giorgio Maggiore at Dusk* (1908–1912). It shows the painter's impression of a sunset in Venice, capturing the transient effects of light and colour, often revisiting and adjusting his canvases over time to achieve the desired impression. A reminder to us all of the wonder and awe available to those who look and allow themselves to see.

While many obsess about extending our lives through diet, sleep, exercise (which are all good things of course), some miss the point. Life enlargement is just as important, perhaps; it's not just about tracking and adding raw

[131] M. Magee and H. O'Brien, '*Sweet Cootehill Town*', YouTube video (posted 2019). Available from www.youtube.com/watch?v=nUQvlsp4qL8

increments of time. It's also about a deeper more enriching purpose, exploring the breadth and depth of human experience.

Marcus's journey led him to a purpose that transcended himself. In our final chapter we move to a discussion of transcendence in a broader context.

15 Transcendence

'Listen to the sound of one hand clapping' – Zen Buddhism[132]

Eudaimonia (Ancient Greece): Aristotle's concept of eudaimonia, often translated as 'flourishing' or 'well-being,' suggests that fulfilment is achieved through the pursuit of virtue, moral character, and the realisation of one's potential.[133]

In the world of sports there unfolded a moment seldom seen – a tableau of beaming faces, the harmonious chorus of laughter and an expansive, amiable throng of spectators. At the helm of this captivating spectacle stood Bill Veeck, the custodian of the Chicago White Sox. Veeck, with conviction in his voice, professed that baseball transcended victory, defeat or even money, for that matter. To him it represented something beyond those things. It was the art of fostering a communal spirit, a medium to unite people in the pursuit of joy, an opportunity to bask in the sheer delight of shared experience.

---

132 E. Hakuin, *The Sound of One Hand: 281 Zen Koans with Answers* (2010). Translated by Yoel Hoffmann.

133 Aristotle, *Nicomachean Ethics* (1998). Translated by W. D. Ross.

Bill Veeck, a man with roots in baseball reaching as far back as the 1940s, possessed an aura uniquely his own by the mid-1970s. The indelible mark of the Second World War had left him one leg short, and yet there he was, amid the throngs at White Sox baseball games, hobbling through the crowd with a demeanour that exuded warmth and benevolence. Bill wore the visage of a kindly grandfather, despite his imposing athletic build. And what truly set him apart was his perpetual smile, which seemed to mirror the very essence of the game he held so dear.

He was an esteemed figure in American Major League Baseball franchise ownership and promotion. He etched his legacy through an unconventional path of hustling and deal-making. Unlike the owners of today, Bill didn't have much money (bringing together consortiums of wealthy investors to buy clubs), particularly in the 1970s. But when he took over the White Sox for the second time in 1975 he had a plan. He and his son Mike were on a mission to pack the stadium to capacity by cultivating an atmosphere of unbridled enjoyment. To achieve this, they innovated. From fireworks displays to introducing the heartwarming tradition of the seventh-inning serenade 'Take Me Out to the Ball Game', the Veecks were pioneers of merriment. Giveaways, promotions and imaginative spectacles became their stock-in-trade.

What set Bill and Mike apart was their relentless pursuit of fun and bringing together. Their experimentation knew no bounds, from the introduction of circus animals to the dramatic spectacle of an exploding scoreboard to herald the triumphant crack of a home run. In an era where baseball ownership was often a pursuit of championships, the Veecks chose a different path – one paved with laughter, wonder and the enduring joy of America's pastime. The fans came not just for baseball but for a joyous experience. It was an approach that Mike later successfully brought to the independent baseball leagues in the 1990s after Bill's death. It's in this context that we'll look at compelling reasons to think beyond ourselves. And it's the pursuit of this type of transcendence that's at the heart of our final chapter, where we'll grapple with some formidable questions and insights. We'll attempt to examine what constitutes the essence of a truly fulfilling life direction and why that's often found in what we can do for others.

Direction

The Britannica dictionary defines transcendence as the ability to 'rise above or go beyond the normal limits'.[134] Setting out to write this book, the task that particularly daunted me was how to finish it. As we approach that point it's useful to recount my goal in writing the book in the first place. That goal was to ask hard questions that I personally wanted answers to. Pushing myself beyond what I perceived were my normal limits in order to find those answers. I also wanted to discover and impart some key understandings for you, the reader, along the way, learned from much wiser people than me. In my personal opinion, having read many books in this area, they can be sometimes a little too goal-driven in the get-rich-quick fashion, or too removed to be of practical use. I hope this book settles in a new place, where the reader can pick it up from time to time and enjoy these real-life stories, as I have in researching and writing them.

On the cover of this book we see a triangle or pyramid structure behind a runner. When I was researching the overarching structure of the book I came upon a concept that blew my mind. The golden ratio: 1.618.[c] This is a mathematical constant often found in nature, art and architecture. The golden ratio (ϕ), some believe, was not only represented in the dimensions of the great pyramids of Egypt but also in the building blocks of life itself.

It's a ratio of a pyramid's height to half the length of its base, which is approximately 1.618. Whether this was intentional or coincidental is a matter of debate. The structure is not just inherently stable, it has allowed many ancient pyramids to survive for millennia, resisting natural disasters and the ravages of time. The golden ratio is also evident in the arrangement of leaves, seeds and branches in plants. This pattern (phyllotaxis) optimizes sunlight exposure. The proportions and patterns in the bodies of various animals, including humans, often exhibit the golden ratio. This is seen in the spiral shapes of shells and the proportions of bird wings, among other things. Some structures in space, such as the spiral arms of galaxies, reflect the golden ratio.

---

[134] *Transcend*, Britannica Dictionary. Available from www.britannica.com/dictionary/transcend [accessed March 2024].

So, as we near the end of our journey together in this book, I hope you'll indulge me for a moment as we return to what I set out to achieve in the Introduction to this book. I want in essence to apply this golden ratio metaphor to my own methodology. The intention at the outset was to establish some base core skills, set out in the initial seven chapters. These are just some, of course, and are represented by the *A*ctivity or actions we can take to address the challenges in our lives, whether those challenges are sought out or thrust upon us. Part 2 of this book indicates a *B*alance necessary to be struck to maintain that positive action in a sustained way, with the observance of personal values and fail-safes for the avoidance of things like burnout.

There's a third point, a point of *C*ongruence, which is in fact a meeting of points A and B. A direction we might find worthwhile moving towards. An optimal point C, which is personal and unique to all of us as individuals. In geometry, if we were to bisect a line from two points at either end, striking two sufficiently arching lines with a compass from these two opposing points, there would be an intersecting point C.[135] This point C in geometry would provide the top point of the pyramid or triangle.

Finding direction in life isn't as simple. I can only be guided by what I think are things worth moving towards. A little more control, purpose and transcendence are probably not a bad start.

We begin this final conversation in the distant past.

Signs of civilization

Margaret Mead, a pioneering anthropologist, spent her career delving deep into the annals of ancient human civilizations to unearth the subtleties of human interaction and compassion. It was her research focused on a point in time at the end of the last ice age that shed light on a profound revelation. A skeleton, with its femur bone healed. Evidence that someone had taken time to stay with an injured person. They had bound up the wound and tended to them through recovery. It was a pivotal divergence from the merciless

[135] In geometry, bisecting a line means dividing the line into two equal parts at its midpoint. When a line segment is bisected, the point of division is equidistant from both endpoints of the segment, effectively creating two segments of equal length. See R. Larson and L. Boswell, *Geometry* (2001).

ways of nature. Helping someone else through difficulty, Mead concluded, is where civilization begins.[136]

Fulfilment

Science tells us that our brains are largely biased towards negative thoughts to ensure our survival. Positive thoughts are nice to have but anxiety, fear, sadness, disgust and so on have kept us alive in the historical sense. It's estimated that 40% of our baseline mood is derived from our genes, while the rest is influenced by environmental factors.[137] Being happy or satisfied is not a permanent state and neither is being unhappy. We're capable of all these emotions but they, of course, don't last. Our body's homeostasis system returns our mood to its normal level over time. The good news is that we can certainly be happier, and being happier is a very worthwhile direction. Harvard professor Arthur C. Brooks runs the Leadership & Happiness Laboratory at the Center for Public Leadership. Brooks, a best-selling author, recommends that we begin with a mission statement for our lives.[138] Who we are, what we want and tangible steps we're going to take to be happier. Before embarking on this step, it's important to understand what types of happiness we might seek.

Hedonic and eudaimonic are two different perspectives on happiness and well-being derived from ancient cultures.

Hedonic happiness

Hedonic happiness or well-being is based on the concept of hedonism, the pursuit of pleasure and the avoidance of pain.[139] This form of happiness is associated with experiencing positive emotions, enjoyment and satisfaction.

---

136 The authenticity of the story has been under debate; however, the author Ira Byock feels that it was correctly attributed to Mead. See I. Byock, *The Best Care Possible: A Physician's Quest to Transform Care Through the End of Life* (2012).

137 M. Pogosyan, 'How genes influence happiness: understanding the link between DNA and well-being' in *Psychology Today* (2019).

138 See, for example, A. Brooks and O. Winfrey, *Build the Life You Want: The Art and Science of Getting Happier* (2023).

139 Further reading: E. Diener *et al.*, 'Beyond the hedonic treadmill: revising the adaptation theory of well-being' in *American Psychologist* 61 (4), 305–314 (2006).

It's about immediate gratification, comfort and the experience of pleasure. Measures of hedonic well-being often focus on how frequently individuals experience positive affect (joy, contentment, etc.) versus negative affect (anxiety, sadness, etc.), and their overall life satisfaction.

We can get satisfaction, but we can't keep satisfaction. This is termed the hedonic treadmill.[140] The treadmill aspect refers to chasing more, and in the material world meets expectations momentarily, but expectations and desires rise in tandem. This results in no permanent gain in happiness.

Eudaimonia

Eudaimonia, by contrast, takes us beyond the fleeting allure of dopamine rushes associated with happiness.[141] Our conventional understanding of happiness often intertwines it with activities that trigger endorphin-driven spikes in dopamine levels. Think of the classic comedy TV series *Father Ted*, where the protagonist, an Irish priest banished to a remote island parish, is often depicted daydreaming about his escape from this predicament. These daydreams transport him to a disco, donning sunglasses and showering money around him – an embodiment of the partying metaphor for happiness.

Reducing happiness to a mere analogy of revelry is, in essence, a limited perspective. Chasing after activities solely for the momentary pleasure they promise often proves to be an ill-fated strategy and perhaps also a contributor to pervasive addiction issues in our world.

The philosopher Aristotle offered an alternative view. He instead argued for the concept of happiness through a solid foundation of underlying well-being: 'eudaimonia'. As noted in the quote at the beginning of this chapter, this is often translated as 'flourishing'. Eudaimonia implies a state of eudaimonic well-being, associated with self-acceptance, personal growth, purpose in life, positive relationships with others and a healthy level of autonomy. This concept is not about how we might feel in one moment or another. We might not feel particularly elated or energetic at any given moment or day but rather

---

[140] P. Brickman and D. Campbell, 'Hedonic Relativism and Planning the Good Society' in *Adaptation-Level Theory: A Symposium*, edited by M. Appley, 287–305 (1971).

[141] Further reading: A. Waterman, 'Reconsidering happiness: a eudaimonist's perspective' in *The Journal of Positive Psychology* 3 (4), 234–252 (2008).

benefit from a strong sense of underlying purpose and meaning in our lives that sustains long-term well-being.

Both perspectives offer valuable insights into the nature of happiness and well-being. Some psychologists argue that a truly happy or satisfying life includes both hedonic and eudaimonic aspects. It's about balancing the pursuit of pleasure with the pursuit of meaning and self-realization. With this in mind, what does this long-term purpose or meaning look like?

Arthur C. Brooks proposes that it's possible to maintain a type of 'happierness', a state of becoming, reaching towards.[142]

Behaviour and needs

Abraham H. Maslow (1908–1970) is one of the most cited and important figures in modern psychology. His best-known work is the hierarchy of needs, which is usually displayed graphically in the form of a pyramid. Essentially, Maslow was a proponent of positive psychology. He dwelled not on treating mentally ill people, but rather focused his research on mentally well people in the context of their needs as human beings. He broke these down into two categories. First, deficiency needs, those that are absent, such as food, shelter, relationship needs and self-esteem. When these were satisfied he posited that what drives us then becomes instead a category of 'growth' needs. In short, the need to be all we can be.

Maslow dedicated many decades to the study of human behaviour. He began his academic and research career in psychology in the 1930s and continued his work until his death in 1970. During this time he made significant contributions to the field, including what he initially saw as the pinnacle of human needs, the concept of self-actualization – fulfilling our personal potential.[143]

While Maslow's theories and contributions to psychology have left a lasting impact, they're not without their detractors.[d] But even with legitimate criticism and cautionary warnings, Maslow manages to give us a framework

---

[142] A. Brooks, *Happierness*, YouTube video (posted May 2021). Available from www.youtube.com/watch?v=C4_UtRiNGZk

[143] A. Maslow, 'A theory of human motivation' in *Psychological Review* 50 (4), 370–396 (1943).

to consider, refine and re-evaluate at a personal level. Interestingly, it's not well known that around 25 years after publishing his hierarchy of needs theory he made another breakthrough in his thinking. He concluded shortly before he died that self-actualization, fulfilling all our potential and being all that we can be, was not the pinnacle of human existence. There may be something more important.

Reaching upwards

Maslow noted in a personal journal entry of 11 June 1967 that the 'ones who are struggling & reaching upward really have a better prognosis than the ones who rest perfectly content at the SA [self-actualized] level'.[144]

There's that word 'reaching' again. 'Reaching' upward? It's possible that he came to a new realization. Perhaps a realization that fulfilling our individual needs did not constitute the ultimate and deeply fulfilling goal of human existence. In an amendment to his initial framework, he posited that the tier above self-actualization was in fact self-transcendence.

It's important at this junction to note that the concept of self-transcendence encompasses various overlapping definitions and interpretations. Viktor Frankl wrote that the 'essentially self-transcendent quality of human existence renders man a being reaching out beyond himself'.[145]

Again we see that word 'reaching'. Self-transcendence, Maslow is perhaps telling us, represents a state of being that goes beyond the pursuit of personal needs and desires. It involves a shift in focus from self-centred concerns to a broader, more altruistic perspective. It's the recognition that there's something greater than the individual self. Furthermore, the act of fulfilment itself is the state of reaching – the attempt to touch or grasp a larger purpose than ourselves.

If we turn for a moment to eastern philosophy, Zen Buddhist monks are taught in ways that include a series of questions and riddles from senior monks, known as Koans. Koans are self-paradoxical riddles used as a meditation discipline. For example, the quote at the beginning of this chapter. When both hands are clapped a sound is produced; so how can we hear the sound of one hand clapping?

---

144 The journals of A. H. Maslow Vol. 2, 798–799 (1979).

145 V. Frankl, *The Will to Meaning: Foundations and Applications of Logotherapy* (2014) [1969].

Typically, there's no one satisfying answer to this type of Koan. They instead point to a clue or fleeting insight. It's thought, however, that this Koan refers to the fact that our individuality is an illusion. We're defined as individuals by our interactions with others. To produce a clapping sound is the interaction of two hands – no sound is produced otherwise.

Empathy

Maslow believed that self-transcendence relies on that interaction with others. Acts of kindness and service to others without expecting anything in return. This can include helping those in need, contributing to the well-being of our neighbours, the community, our world.

This last point is important, because throughout history a focus on tribal or local community interests at the expense of those further afield has fuelled dangerous and divisive actions. Humanity's greatest atrocities have come from viewing the needs of our own tribe over others, at times viewing other tribes as somehow less human.[146] Maslow's point was perhaps about not just acting in the interests of our neighbours and local communities but rather striking an equilibrium with our fellow men/women and the delicate environmental and planetary ecosystem we all depend upon. It represents a shift from a self-centred orientation to a more selfless and holistic perspective, which can lead to a deeper sense of purpose and contentment.

This has significant application in world affairs. Robert S. McNamara, who we referred to in Chapter 1, was a significant figure in the global history of the 20th century, holding several key positions throughout his life. He was president of Ford Motor Company, and US Secretary of Defense under Presidents John F. Kennedy and Lyndon B. Johnson from 1961 to 1968, during the Cuban Missile Crisis and the escalation of the Vietnam War. He was very influential and played a crucial role in shaping US military strategy and policymaking during this tumultuous period in world history. He later also became president of the World Bank. His legacy is complex, particularly regarding his role in the Vietnam War, which, at the age of around 86 years old, he reflected on

[146] Dehumanization is a common before atrocities, where targeted groups are portrayed as less than human to justify violence against them. This tactic was evident in the Holocaust, and the Rwandan, Bosnian and Cambodian genocides, where it facilitated mass violence by diminishing empathy and moral barriers.

critically, in *The Fog of War* documentary.[147] He also wrote on the subject in his 1995 book, *In Retrospect: The Tragedy and Lessons of Vietnam.* We have to be mindful here that it's sometimes human nature to reflect on our personal history in a revisionist self-serving way.

Nevertheless, McNamara recounts how the US had misjudged the geopolitical intentions of adversaries such as Vietnam. The documentary covers a meeting with his opposite number, the former foreign minister of Vietnam, Nguyễn Cơ Thạch. This 1995 meeting was significant because it allowed McNamara to gain new insights and perspectives on the Vietnam War. He recounted how this meeting confirmed a long-standing fear. The fear that the US had in fact fundamentally misunderstood Vietnam's objectives. In retrospect, McNamara concludes that Vietnam simply wanted independence, something the US missed. The US saw Vietnam simply as a pawn of the Russians and Chinese. McNamara uses the word empathy again and again in failures of foreign policy – that he was very much a part of. He concludes, more or less, that they had failed to make a transcendence, a shift from a self-centred orientation, to listen and understand their adversaries. 'I formed the hypothesis that each of us [US and Vietnam] could have achieved our objectives without the war.'[148] Unfortunately, of course, millions died in the Vietnam War, which lasted over 19 years.

What Maslow and McNamara had in common was a realization they both encountered and documented towards the end of their lives. Significantly, both men had the courage to challenge their own previous convictions and articulate them, with implications, especially as far as McNamara is concerned, for his own enduring legacy.

Hopefully sharing some of these thoughts can help us connect with the importance of taking the time to understand others, in order to help us get past the limits of our own understanding. Maslow saw the act of self-transcendence as an 'end in itself', the reaching of a state of being that has inherent value and is worth pursuing for its own sake. It isn't pursued for selfish reasons or as a means to an end, but rather as an intrinsic source of joy, meaning and fulfilment in life. It's the 'struggling and reaching upward' that creates the intrinsic value of ultimate fulfilment.

---

[147] E. Morris, director, *The Fog of War: Eleven Lessons from the Life of Robert S. McNamara.* Sony Pictures Classics (2003).

[148] Ibid. See 'Lesson #7: Belief and seeing are both often wrong.'

Bill Veeck, towards the end of his life, got what many others do not, a second chance. He reacquired ownership of the White Sox for a second time in 1975. Aside from making enough money to keep the lights on, Bill and his son Mike became animated by a goal and a mission that transcended the boundaries of self-interest and commerce. They had stumbled upon a grander destination, the pursuit of 'happierness' in bringing people together, which changed the sport forever.

Conclusion

Considering that grander destination for a moment, it would be remiss not to think of Christopher McCandless and his remarkable journey 'into the wild'.[149] In the book and movie of the same title, he travelled across North America and eventually hitchhiked to Alaska in April 1992. There he entered the Alaskan bush with minimal supplies, hoping to live simply off the land and experience nature. The wilderness can be a powerful source of inspiration and learning, offering insights into natural processes, biodiversity and the interconnectedness of life. He took inspiration from authors such as Jack London and Henry David Thoreau, who celebrated the beauty of nature, simplicity and self-reliance. He eventually settled on the eastern bank of the Sushana river, where he found an abandoned bus to use as a makeshift shelter. The exact circumstances leading to his untimely death are unclear. The prevailing theory suggests that he became increasingly weak and unable to gather enough food to sustain himself, perhaps as a result of eating toxic seeds in the area.

He journalled his final thoughts before his tragic death, and I would like to leave the final reference in this book to him. It was a powerful final entry, discovered after his death, which read: 'An unshared happiness is not happiness.'[150]

Just as perhaps in the same way, an unshared success is not success.

---

[149] J. Krakauer, *Into the Wild* (2011).

[150] Chapter 16 of *Into the Wild* delves into the final days of Christopher McCandless's life and his reflections, as interpreted through the lens of the notes and annotations he left behind in his books and the journal he maintained during his time in the wild.

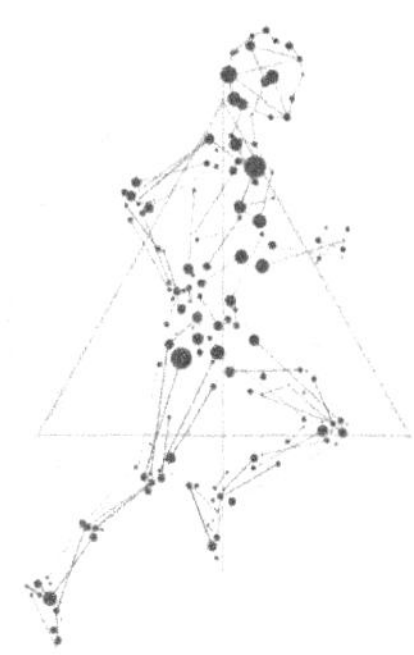

Endnotes

[a] Professional athletes, in particular, learn how to get the best out of themselves. In the early 1990s Michael Jordan, a colossus of the basketball world, faced off against Le Bradford Smith, a relatively unheralded guard for the Washington Bullets. In their first encounter Smith performed exceptionally well, outscoring Jordan. This performance was perceived by Jordan as a personal slight against him, specifically a claim that Smith had boasted about his performance, saying something to the effect of 'nice game, Mike'. It was a challenge to his dominance on the court. In their next meeting Jordan was a force unleashed, scoring a phenomenal 36 points in the first half alone, just one point short of Smith's total point-scoring in their previous game. It was later revealed that Jordan had fabricated a part of the narrative – the comment by Smith hadn't really happened. It did, however, serve as a catalyst for Jordan. This incident is a classic example of how elite athletes like Jordan manufacture motivation from perceived slights, real or imagined. He used this narrative, whether factual or not, to get angry, to fuel his competitive fire. It shows us how motivation, even derived from the most personal and sometimes imagined sources, can drive individuals to extraordinary heights.

[b] A very relevant comparison with Leeson in this context is Jordan Belfort, the US fraudulent trader and the subject of the book and movie, *The Wolf of Wall Street.* In this regard, Belfort himself once said, 'You know, nothing is ever enough for me' (Jordan Belfort – *White Collar Criminal*, www.documentarytube.com/environmental/

jordan-belfort-white-collar-criminal/). He went on to describe in the same conversation that the driveway of the mansion he had just bought wasn't long enough, he felt he needed to add to it. Belfort, like Leeson, was also from humble beginnings and somewhat of an outsider in the stockbroker world of New York. Being from a Jewish background that he appeared to be somewhat embarrassed about, he spent most of his career trying to be accepted into the conservative protestant circles that ran much of the financial sector he was involved in. He had exceptional sales skills such as persuasion, and a word that comes up again and again is charisma. He used these skills, however, to ultimately create a business aggressively selling sub-par stocks in poorly run or in some cases non-existent businesses at exorbitant commissions, later floating companies and breaching many SEC rules, resulting in a lengthy prison sentence.

[c] The Golden Ratio, a concept revered for its aesthetic harmony, traces its roots back to Ancient Greece, notably through Euclid's definition in his 'Elements' and its speculated presence in Greek architecture, such as the Parthenon. Its significance was possibly acknowledged earlier by the Pythagoreans and also discussed by Plato in relation to universal beauty. In the Middle Ages, Fibonacci's sequence offered an approximation of the ratio, a concept later embraced during the Renaissance, where it was extensively applied in art and architecture, exemplified by Leonardo da Vinci's use of it in his works, such as the *Vitruvian Man*. See M. Livio, *The Golden Ratio: The Story of Phi, the World's Most Astonishing Number* (2002).

[d] Like many theories, critics have expressed concerns and cautionary warnings regarding Maslow's hierarchy of needs. First, they question its empirical foundation, highlighting its reliance on personal observations and case studies, which potentially diminishes its scientific validity and measurability. Second, cultural bias is a pressing issue, with critics arguing that the hierarchy may favour Western individualistic values over collectivist cultures, undermining its universal applicability. Third, rigidity in the hierarchy's structure fails to account for the dynamic and multifaceted nature of human needs, as individuals often pursue multiple needs concurrently, with varied priorities. Moreover, the theory tends to overlook contextual factors influencing needs, and its concept of self-actualization is seen as vague and challenging to quantify. In contemporary psychology, alternative

frameworks such as self-determination theory and positive psychology have overshadowed Maslow's work, relegating it to a secondary role. Critics also argue that the hierarchy oversimplifies human motivation, potentially neglecting individual differences and the complex factors shaping needs and desires.

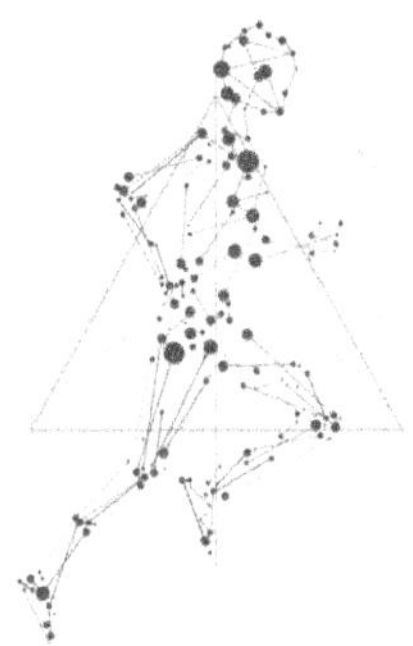

About the Author

Originally a criminal solicitor, Irish author Adrian Kelly has had a number of careers from entrepreneurial work in the renewable energy industry to, more recently, business training and consultancy services with big law firms and governmental agencies. He loves movies and spending time with his family and is a huge sports fan.

He has a broad spectrum of sports coaching experience, from Senior Intercounty Ladies Gaelic Football to amateur Baseball both domestically and internationally with the U18 Irish International Team at two European Championships. Academically, he has lectured and been an external examiner at the Law Society of Ireland and is currently undertaking a master's degree in psychology. He speaks at business conferences and wellness events on subjects ranging from motivation and performance to life direction. He also works closely with a number of high schools, pioneering Dragon's Den competitions for students and overseeing a college scholarship programme. For more information or details on how to get in touch, see www.askmore.ie.

His overarching goal is to help people get the most out of themselves and life.

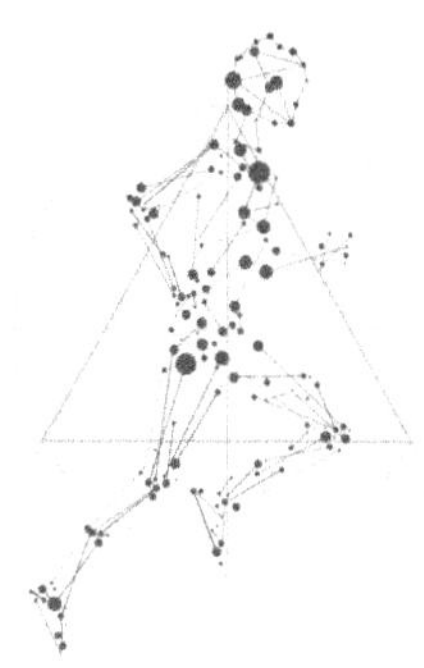

Index

www.ingramcontent.com/pod-product-compliance
Lightning Source LLC
Chambersburg PA
CBHW050030090426
42735CB00021B/3428

* 9 7 8 1 7 8 8 6 0 3 7 9 9 *